The Knowledge Deficit

Books by E. D. Hirsch, Jr.

The Knowledge Deficit

The Schools We Need and Why We Don't Have Them

Books to Build On

The Core Knowledge Series (7 volumes; Kindergarten
   to Grade Six)

Cultural Literacy: What Every American Needs to Know

The Philosophy of Composition

The Aims of Interpretation

Validity in Interpretation

Innocence and Experience: An Introduction to Blake

Wordsworth and Schelling: A Typological Study
   of Romanticism

Edited by E. D. Hirsch, Jr.

The New First Dictionary of Cultural Literacy
   (with associate editors William G. Rowland, Jr.,
   and Michael Stanford)

The New Dictionary of Cultural Literacy
   (with Joseph F. Kett and James Trefil)

The
KNOWLEDGE
DEFICIT

CLOSING THE SHOCKING EDUCATION GAP
FOR AMERICAN CHILDREN

E. D. HIRSCH, JR.

HOUGHTON MIFFLIN COMPANY
BOSTON · NEW YORK

First Houghton Mifflin paperback edition 2007

Visit our Web site: www.hmhco.com

Library of Congress Cataloging-in-Publication Data
Hirsch, E. D. (Eric Donald).
The knowledge deficit : closing the shocking education gap
for American children / E. D. Hirsch, Jr.
p.   cm.
Includes index.
ISBN-13: 978-0-618-65731-5
ISBN-10: 0-618-65731-2
1. Reading. 2. Reading — United States. 3. Literacy — United States.
4. Education — United States — Philosophy.   I. Title.
LB1050.H567 2006 428.4′071 — DC22 2005023075

ISBN-13: 978-0-618-87225-1 (pbk.)
ISBN-10: 0-618-87225-6 (pbk.)

Printed in the United States of America

DOH 10 9 8 7
4500569285

FOR ELIZA,

who hasn't yet started school —
may this book help make her time
there rich and productive

One of the major contributions of psychology is the recognition [that] . . . much of the information needed to understand a text is not provided by the information expressed in the text itself but must be drawn from the language user's knowledge of the person, objects, states of affairs, or events the discourse is about.

—T. A. VAN DIJK AND W. KINTSCH
Strategies of Discourse Comprehension

I am sure that the power of vested interests is vastly exaggerated compared with the gradual encroachment of ideas . . . Soon or late, it is ideas, not vested interests, which are dangerous for good or evil.

—J. M. KEYNES
*The General Theory of Employment,
Interest, and Money*

Contents

PREFACE   xi

1. WHY DO WE HAVE A KNOWLEDGE DEFICIT?   1

    The Achievement Crisis   1
    The Curse of Romantic Ideas   3
    Should Schooling Be Natural?   7
    What About "Mere Facts"?   8
    Is Knowing How Better than Knowing What?   11
    Is Society to Blame?   14
    Making Better Ideas Prevail   16

2. SOUNDING OUT: JUST THE BEGINNING OF READING   23

    What We've Recently Achieved   23
    Is Reading Like Listening?   26
    Filling in the Blanks   35
    Are Some Kinds of Knowledge Better than Others?   39
    Reading Strategies: A Path to Boredom   45

3. KNOWLEDGE OF LANGUAGE   51

    Learning the Standard Language   51
    Learning Grammar   54
    Learning the Elaborated Code   56
    Building Vocabulary   58
    Can Disadvantaged Children Catch Up?   66

4. KNOWLEDGE OF THINGS   68

    What the Text Doesn't Say 68
    Who Is the General Reader? 70
    How Much Knowledge Do We Need? 73
    Which Knowledge Do We Need? 74
    Why Not in the Reading Program? 77

5. USING SCHOOL TIME PRODUCTIVELY   80

    Wasting Students' Time 80
    Blaming Teachers 83
    Better Use of Time Leads to Greater Fairness 85
    Using Time Effectively 88

6. USING TESTS PRODUCTIVELY   91

    Are Tests Driving Our Schools? 91
    The Flaws of State Tests 93
    The Nature of Reading Tests 96
    What Kinds of Tests Will Enhance Education? 102

7. ACHIEVING COMMONALITY AND FAIRNESS   107

    Reading and a Wider Crisis 107
    Fulfilling Our Nation's Highest Ideals 108
    Constantly Changing Schools — A Critical Issue 109
    Localism and a Perfect Storm of Bad Educational Ideas 112
    Are There Decisive Advantages in Specifying Definite
        Content? 115
    Thinking the Unthinkable: A Core of Common Content
        in Early Grades 119

    APPENDIX: THE CRITICAL IMPORTANCE OF AN ADEQUATE
        THEORY OF READING   127
    NOTES   139
    ACKNOWLEDGMENTS   159
    INDEX   161

Preface

This book offers solutions to the related problems of low reading abilities in American children and the needlessly wide achievement gaps between ethnic and racial groups. As I edit the book, I see a report in the *Washington Post* that carries this headline: "Schools Shift Approach as Adolescent Readers Fail to Improve." The gist of the article is that nine-year-olds have measurably improved in speed and accuracy at sounding out words, but thirteen-year-olds have not shown any advance in reading comprehension—a result that is forecast and explained here. Although the experts interviewed for the *Post* article say that we should expend more effort on these thirteen-year-olds—for instance, enrolling them in "power literacy" classes—such efforts will certainly fail unless schooling is radically changed in the grades before middle school. By the same token, the renewed emphasis on high school will yield similarly disappointing results for similar reasons. Anyone who digests the following pages will come to understand that the reading problems of middle school do not lie in middle school at all, nor those of high school in high school.

To bring all children to reading proficiency and at the same time narrow the academic gap between racial and ethnic groups are goals that have eluded American schools for too long. This book explains why universal educational achievement with equity *is* possible but also why it cannot be accomplished overnight. We now understand in some detail why children's acquisition of knowledge and vocabulary is necessarily slow and gradual. Yet despite this inherent gradualness, we can greatly accelerate the achievements of all students if we adopt knowledge-oriented modes of schooling that use school time effectively, and if we abandon process-oriented notions like "reading comprehension strategies" that waste precious school time. The only way to attain the long-desired educational goal of high achievement with fairness to all students is through a structure in which each grade, especially grades one through five, builds knowledge cumulatively (and without boring repetitions) upon the preceding grade. That structure has been lacking in the United States since the 1940s, mainly because one set of ideas has triumphed over another. The importance of ideas and the importance of knowledge are twin themes of this book.

Recently educators have deplored the unfairness of the "digital divide," a phrase used to signify a gap between students who have ready access to computers and those who do not. But while we strive to overcome such unfairness in material distribution, we should not overlook the much more significant unfairness of the *knowledge* gap between children from different economic strata. (Nor should we overlook the other knowledge gap, here called the "knowledge deficit," between the majority of American students and those who attend more coherent systems of schooling in other nations.) Universal access to computers does not by itself go very far in fostering the democratic ideal of making all students competent irrespective of their social backgrounds. If we had a choice between offering each child a computer and imparting to each the broad knowledge that enables a person to use a computer intelligently, we should unhesitatingly choose knowledge.

The book is directed to a general audience as well as to professionals in education. Both groups need to be addressed to help foster significant educational reform. Parents and citizens have the political power to insist on altering received ideas and practices, since without wide public support, no significant educational reform can occur.

But in the end, it is the professionals — teachers and administrators — who will carry out the reform. For these experts I have provided generous footnotes to the relevant research. Both groups want the same result — citizens who are well educated and competent regardless of economic, ethnic, or racial background.

One of the big ways in which we Americans distinguished ourselves from Europe when we created a nation was by adopting the egalitarian idea that great discrepancies in one's life chances should not be the result of who one's parents happen to be. The ideal of a "career open to talents" has been one of the most inspiriting ideals in democracies generally and in the United States especially. From the start we rejected inherited titles and aristocracy. Thomas Jefferson urged the Virginia legislature to abolish primogeniture — the principle that the advantaged oldest son automatically inherits everything. If we fail in our traditional aim of providing equal opportunity to all children at the beginning of life, we fail in our duty to preserve what is best in our inheritance, and we squander the profoundest source of our influence in the wider world. President Reagan was right to use John Winthrop's image of America as a "city on a hill" in order to suggest that the ultimate source of our strength and safety is the power of the example that we set when we live up to our ideals.

The Knowledge Deficit

1

WHY DO WE HAVE A
KNOWLEDGE DEFICIT?

THE ACHIEVEMENT CRISIS

THE PUBLIC SEES that something is badly amiss in the education of our young people. Employers now often need to rely on immigrants from Asia and Eastern Europe to do the math that our own high school graduates cannot do. We score low among developed nations in international comparisons of science, math, and reading. This news is in fact more alarming than most people realize, since our students perform relatively worse on international comparisons the longer they stay in our schools. In fourth grade, American students score ninth in reading among thirty-five countries, which is respectable. By tenth grade they score fifteenth in reading among twenty-seven countries, which is not promising at all for their (and our) economic future.[1] In the global age, a person's and a nation's economic success depend on high reading and/or math ability. We have learned from the phenomenon of outsourcing that those who have these abilities can find a place in the global economy no matter where they happen to live, while those who lack them can be marginalized even if they live in the middle of the United States.

That this crisis in American competence should have been a topic during a recent presidential campaign, even in the midst of terror threats, is a striking sign of its present importance to the American people — of our growing sense that we, like other peoples these days, must live by our wits. The reason that reading ability is the heart of the matter is that reading ability correlates with learning and communication ability. Reading proficiency isn't in and of itself the magic key to competence. It's what reading enables us to learn and to do that is critical. In the information age, the key to economic and political achievement is the ability to gain new knowledge rapidly through reading and listening.

The public's estimate of the great importance of reading skill is strongly supported by the research evidence. Students' scores in reading comprehension are consistently associated with their subsequent school grades and their later economic success. Under our current educational methods, a child's reading in second grade reliably predicts that child's academic performance in eleventh grade, quite irrespective of his or her native talent and diligence.[2] Long-range studies show that if children become skilled readers, the United States offers them a fair chance in life — probably more so than any other nation.[3] But that is a big if. Becoming a skilled reader — a skilled user of language — is not fast or easy. If it were, our schools would be enabling all our students to reach this goal, when in fact they are bringing fewer than half of them to reading proficiency.

Verbal SAT scores in the United States took a nosedive in the 1960s, and since then they have remained flat. Despite intense efforts by the schools, reading scores nationwide have remained low. An equally worrisome outcome of current school methods and the knowledge deficit they cause is the continuation of the large reading gap between demographic groups. While the origins of the discrepancy lie outside school, in the language that toddlers hear, our current educational methods have not been able to narrow that early gap, but instead have allowed it to widen as students move through the grades. Over the past decades, we have made little progress in bringing all social groups to a reasonable proficiency in reading comprehension. The average reading scores of Hispanics have hovered some twenty-five points below that of whites, while scores of blacks are nearly thirty points below that of whites. These large gaps tell only part of the story: whites cannot read well either. More than half of them — some 59 percent — fail to read at a proficient level. For Hispanics, it is a depressing 85 percent, and for blacks it is a tragic 88 percent.[4]

. *Tragic* is not too strong a word. Reading ability correlates with almost everything that a democratic education aims to provide, including the ability to be an informed citizen who can actively participate in the self-government of a democracy. What gives the reading gap between demographic groups a special poignancy is the dramatic failure of our schools to live up to the basic ideal of a democratic education, which, as Thomas Jefferson conceived it, is the ideal of offering all children the opportunity to succeed, regardless of who their parents happen to be. Reading proficiency is at the very heart of the democratic educational enterprise, and is rightly called the "new civil rights frontier."[5]

THE CURSE OF ROMANTIC IDEAS

The reason for this state of affairs — tragic for millions of students as well as for the nation — is that an army of American educators and reading experts are fundamentally wrong in their ideas about education and especially about reading comprehension. Their well-intentioned yet mistaken views are the significant reason (more than other constantly blamed factors, even poverty) that many of our children are not attaining reading proficiency, thus crippling their later schooling. An understanding of how these mistaken ideas arose may help us to overcome them.

When I began college teaching in the 1950s, my academic specialty was the history of ideas. I also specialized in the theory of textual interpretation, which, reduced to its essence, is the theory of reading. So I became well versed in the scientific literature on language comprehension and in American and British intellectual history of the nineteenth century. This double research interest prepared my mind for disturbing insights about American schooling. I saw that John Maynard Keynes's remark about the power of ideas over vested interests which I have used as an epigraph was profoundly right. Root ideas are much more important in practical affairs than we usually realize, especially when they are so much taken for granted that they are hidden from our view.

As I taught intellectual history, with a focus on writers like William Blake and William Wordsworth, my immersion in nineteenth-century romanticism gave me another insight into what had gone wrong in our schools. Our nation was born in the Enlightenment but bred in the Romantic period. Today we most often use the term *romantic* to refer to romantic love. But romanticism as a broad intellectual movement that has greatly influenced American thought has much less to do with romantic love than with a complacent faith in the benefits of nature. Such faith was the aspect of nineteenth-century ideas that powerfully influenced our young nation in its beginnings, and it still dominates our thinking about education and many other things.

Consider the idea that school learning, including reading, is or should be natural. The word *natural* has been a term of honor in our country ever since our forebears elevated "nature" and "natural" to a status that had earlier been occupied by divine law. Following the Colonial period, during the heady days of the early 1800s, the most influential thinkers in New England were no longer writers like Jonathan Edwards, who had exhorted us to follow the commandments of God's law, but writers like Emerson and Thoreau, who admonished us to develop ourselves according to nature. That was a hugely important shift in our mental orientation. Vernon Parrington titled the second volume of his massive intellectual history of the United States *The Romantic Revolution in America, 1800–1860,* and his use of the term *revolution* accurately estimates the fundamental change that took place in the American attitude to nature and to education.[6]

The fundamental idea of romanticism is that there isn't any boundary between the natural and the divine. Jonathan Edwards emphatically did not see nature and the natural as being either reliable or divine. In his famous 1741 sermon called "Sinners in the Hands of an Angry God," he cautions us against the sinful "natural man" and contrasts an imperfect "nature" with divine "grace," which is a special supernatural dispensation that sinful "natural man" must seek if he is to be saved.[7] In the nineteenth century, by contrast, American Romantics like Emerson, Whitman, and even our great educational reformer Horace Mann thought that if you followed nature, in life and in education, you really were following the divine. There were no natural sinners. Sin was a product of civilization. "Nature never did betray the heart that loved her," as Wordsworth wrote. To be natural was automatically to be good, whether in life or in learning.

Horace Mann is justly praised as the father of public education in the United States, and he rightly saw the need of our schools to bring all children, including recent immigrants, into the main stream of American life. But romantic ideas, especially the idea that nature is best, influenced his belief that the best way to teach early reading — sounding out words from the printed page — is by a "natural," whole-word approach.[8] The most important American thinkers of the nineteenth and early twentieth centuries, those who formed our current ways of approaching education and many other matters, believed that the natural cannot lead us astray. Today, when we invoke the word *natural* in this way, we continue to illustrate the powerful influence of romanticism on our thought.

Of course, historians don't always call these ideas romanticism. They have given them special American names. They call Emerson and Thoreau "Transcendentalists." They call John Dewey, the father of present-day American education, a "pragmatist" or a "progressive." But progressivism in education is just another name for romanticism. Within Dewey's writings about education beats the heart of a romantic, as indicated by his continual use of the terms *development* and *growth* with regard to the schooling of children — terms that came as naturally to him as they still do to us. In fact, they come to us so unbidden that we do not even notice the fact that conceiving of education as "growth" on the analogy of a bush or tree is in many cases highly questionable, and is made to seem plausible only because children do indeed develop naturally, both physically and mentally, during the early years of schooling.[9] Being trained in the history of ideas, I had become familiar with the way in which unnoticed metaphors like "growth" and "development" unconsciously govern our thought — and continue to do so, even when scientific evidence clearly shows that reading and doing math are not natural developments at all.

My academic specialties thus freed me to think in new ways about what had gone wrong in our schools and to write my 1987 book, *Cultural Literacy*, which became a surprise bestseller. It was an enormously controversial book. Many classroom teachers and parents praised it as accurately describing the way in which knowledge-oriented teaching had vanished from the early grades. But coming at the height of fierce debates over multiculturalism and gender politics, it was damned with great hostility by cultural reformers and education professors as a reactionary tract aimed at preserving the intellectual domination of white Anglo-Saxon males, and as a means of boring children with mindless drills and stuffing them with "mere facts."

Its main argument, that reading comprehension — literacy itself — depends on specific background knowledge, was overlooked in the cultural taking of sides. The atmosphere seems different today. The intensity of identity politics has diminished. Existing instructional practices have not been working. National mandatory testing, which prods schools to achieve "adequate yearly progress" in reading, has highlighted the bankruptcy of prevailing ideas. The public increasingly understands that the knowledge deficit is a profound failure of social justice. Less understood is the fact that this failure is the consequence of good intentions in the service of inadequate ideas.

SHOULD SCHOOLING BE NATURAL?

The word *nature* has its root in the Latin word *natus* — birth, what organisms are born with. By the same token, the word *development* means an unfolding in time of what at birth we potentially contain. Yet the romantic concept of education as a natural unfolding — by far the most influential idea in the history of American education — has small basis in reality when it comes to reading, writing, and arithmetic. On current scientific evidence, the notion that the job of the schools is to foster the natural development of the child is only a half-truth.[10]

Let's ponder "development" for a moment. When a fertilized egg turns into an embryo, that development is indeed something that unfolds naturally. Similarly, in the first two years of life, when a child learns to walk and talk, those are natural developments that are universal in all cultures. Since the child acquires these extremely difficult skills often without conscious adult instruction, we might mistakenly extend trust in natural unfolding to the next stage of life, when a child enters school. And indeed, that is what educators do when they delay teaching the mechanics of reading until a child reaches a state that is deemed to be a developmental stage of "reading readiness." Before that time, children are not to be interfered with by premature and artificial teaching of letter-sound correspondences, because these are "developmentally inappropriate."

Extreme advocates of this viewpoint insist that children will learn to read as readily as they learned to talk. Similarly, the romantic complacency of American educational thought holds that children, given time, will develop a readiness to understand place value in arithmetic. The idea that children might naturally develop a readiness for either place value or the phonic code overlooks the glaring fact that we as a species might never have invented these things at all. Place value in base-ten arithmetic was a very unnatural invention of civilization that reached Europe even later than the alphabet did

— not until around the fifteenth century.[11] Alphabetic writing was a brilliant, momentous invention, and it was equally unnatural. Scholars are still debating whether or not alphabetic writing was invented only once in human history.[12]

If early childhood experts, liberated from the romantic traditions of American schools, had considered the matter from a historical or anthropological angle, they might have taken stock of the fact that reading is developmentally inappropriate at *all* ages of human life. There is little in the human organism that prepares us naturally for alphabetic reading and writing (decoding and encoding), which have been very late and rare attainments of civilization. The inherent unnaturalness of learning to read is part of the reason that it is at first so difficult and, for many, so painful. Shakespeare memorably captured the perennial unnaturalness of schooling in his picture of the "whining schoolboy" "creeping unwillingly to school."

WHAT ABOUT "MERE FACTS"?

A naturalistic approach to teaching phonics, under the idea that children are somehow wired to master the alphabetic code, is not, however, the most deleterious influence of romantic ideas in hindering the effective teaching of reading. The word *reading* has two senses, often confusingly lumped together. The first means the process of turning printed marks into sounds and these sounds into words. But the second sense means the very different process of understanding those words. Learning how to read in the first sense — decoding through phonics — does not guarantee learning how to read in the second sense — comprehending the meaning of what is read. To become a good comprehender, a child needs a great deal of knowledge. A romantically inspired, long delay in teaching phonics, until children are supposedly developmentally ready, as regrettable as it is, is not nearly as permanently harmful to our students economically and socially as the other aspect of the romantic tradition in education — its knowledge-withholding, anti-intellectual aspect.

Disparagement of factual knowledge as found in books has been a strong current in American thought since the time of Emerson. Henry Ford's famous dictum "History is bunk" is a succinct example. Since the nineteenth century, such anti-intellectualism has been as American as apple pie, as the great historian Richard Hofstadter has pointed out, and it came straight out of the Romantic movement into our schools.[13]

In our pre-romantic days, books were seen as the key to education. In a 1785 letter to his nephew, Peter Carr, aged fifteen, Jefferson recommended that he read books (in the original languages and in this order) by the following authors: Herodotus, Thucydides, Xenophon, Anabasis, Arian, Quintus Curtius, Diodorus Siculus, and Justin. On morality, Jefferson recommended books by Epictetus, Plato, Cicero, Antoninus, Seneca, and Xenophon's *Memorabilia*, and in poetry Virgil, Terence, Horace, Anacreon, Theocritus, Homer, Euripides, Sophocles, Milton, Shakespeare, Ossian, Pope, and Swift.[14] Jefferson's plan of book learning was modest compared to the proper Puritan education of the seventeenth century as advocated by John Milton.[15]

The Romantics rejected such advice. They opposed the reading of books as unnatural, as arising from the artificial habits and constraints of civilization. Wordsworth wrote:

> One impulse from a vernal wood
> Can teach us more of man
> Of moral evil and of good
> Than all the sages can.

Emerson claimed that the farm was a better teacher than the school: "We are shut up in schools and college recitation rooms for ten or fifteen years & come out at last with a bellyful of words & do not know a thing . . . The farm, the farm is the right school . . . The farm is a piece of the world, the School house is not."[16] John Dewey's Lab School, which he started in Chicago in 1896, was based on the conviction that children would learn what they needed by engaging in practical activities such as cooking.

Today our schools and colleges of education, the inheritors of these ideas, are still the nerve centers of an anti-intellectual tradition. One of their most effective rhetorical tics is to identify the acquisition of broad knowledge with "rote learning" of "mere facts" — in subtle disparagement of "merely verbal" presentation in books and through the coherent explanations of teachers. Just like Rousseau, Wordsworth, and Dewey, our schools of education hold that unless school knowledge is connected to "real life" in a "hands-on" way, it is unnatural and dead; it is "rote" and "meaningless." It consists of "mere facts." But nobody advocates rote learning of disconnected facts. Neither Milton nor Thomas Jefferson nor any of their more thoughtful contemporaries who championed book learning advocated rote learning. What they did advocate was the systematic acquisition of broad knowledge. And such knowledge is precisely what it takes to become a good reader. Our unwarranted faith in nature — in the idea that so essential and unnatural a skill as decoding will occur mainly through natural development, or that needed knowledge will be imbibed naturally through hands-on experience, plus our faith that how-to strategies will lead to reading competence — have led to the mistaken dogma that reading is a formal skill that can be transferred from one task to another regardless of subject matter.

The factual knowledge that is found in books is the key to reading comprehension. A deficit of factual knowledge and the deficit in language it entails are the causes of the so-called fourth-grade slump that many children experience.[17] For some time now, researchers have observed this phenomenon. Jane scores well in reading in grades one through three but surprisingly begins to score badly in grade four. That's not because Jane suddenly took a backward step. It's because in the early grades she was mainly learning how to decode the printed marks easily and fluently, as reflected in her rising test scores. But in grade four, when Jane was given more challenging content to read in class and on tests, her limited comprehension of language began to show. It was not her fault. Her comprehension problem had been there but had gone unrecognized and untreated in the earlier grades. By fourth grade it is very late to correct it — a tragedy, because this failure most seriously limits her progress in later elementary grades, in middle school, in high school, and in later life. Children who lag in comprehension in early grades tend to fall even further behind in later years.[18] For children to make substantial progress in reading, they must make early and substantial progress in knowledge.

Is Knowing How Better than Knowing What?

If "mere facts" do not matter as much to the romantics as "real-world" experiences, and if book learning and a "bellyful of words" are not essential to education, then what is essential to education? Professional educators had to find some answer to justify schooling at all (*pace* Emerson), and they found it in the notion that certain subjects, like reading and math, are all-purpose, formal skills which, once learned, can be applied to all subjects and problems. This answer was given not only by the Romantics in the nineteenth and early twentieth centuries but also by their successors in our education schools today — that *how-to knowledge,* skills that are universally applicable to all circumstances of life, is the important thing to be learned. The various schools of "progressive" educational thinkers have agreed on this point. A specific, factual curriculum, they hold, is not needed for gaining all-purpose cognitive skills and strategies.[19] Instead of burdening our minds with a lot of dead facts, we should become expert in solving problems, in thinking critically — in reading fluently — and then we will be able to learn anything we need.

This idea, which I have called formalism, has a plausible sound to it. (If it did not seem reasonable and sound, it could not have so thoroughly captured the American mind.) Its surface plausibility derives from the fact that a good education can indeed create skilled readers and critical thinkers. The mistake is to think that these achievements are the result of formal, all-purpose skills rather than abilities that are completely dependent on broad factual knowledge. While it is true that proficient reading and critical thinking are all-purpose abilities, they are not content-independent, formal skills at all but are always based on concrete, relevant knowledge and cannot be exercised apart from what psychologists call "domain-specific" knowledge. The only thing that transforms reading skill and critical thinking skill into general all-purpose abilities is a person's possession of general, all-purpose knowledge.[20]

Formalism in reading is the notion, powerfully dominant in our schools, that reading comprehension is a skill, like typing, that can be transferred from one text to another. Comprehension skill is said to depend on formal "comprehension strategies," such as "predicting, summarizing, questioning, and clarifying." This innocent-seeming idea affects classes all over the nation, depriving them of substance and intellectual structure.

Here's an example of how it affects real children in real classrooms. In May 2004, a front-page story in the *Washington Post* described the activities in a third-grade classroom at a public school in Maryland, which the reporter, Linda Perlstein, identified as being typical of activities "across the nation." Perlstein had been sitting in classrooms at the school, observing what went on and talking to students, teachers, and administrators. Her long report is useful reading for anybody who is interested in the practical consequences for American children of formalistic ideas about reading.[21]

The piece begins with a comment by one of the students:

> Here is 9-year-old Zulma Berrios's take on the school day: "In the morning we read. Then we go to Mrs. Witthaus and read. Then after lunch we read. Then we read some more."

These reading periods, Perlstein points out, come at the expense of classes in history, science, and art. The reading materials themselves are quite vapid. In this particular class, the children were reading a book about a grasshopper storm. But the point of the class was not to learn anything in depth about grasshoppers; the point was to learn how to ferret meaning out of a text by using formal "strategies."

> For 50 minutes, Tracey Witthaus pulls out a small group of third-graders — including Zulma — for Soar to Success, an intensive reading-comprehension program used at many county schools. Instead of studying school desegregation and the anniversary of *Brown* v. *Board of Education,* Zulma's group finishes a book about a grasshopper storm and practices reading strategies: predict, summarize, question, clarify. "Clarify," said Zulma, who began the year reading at the late first-grade level. "When I come to a word I don't know, I look for chunks I do. Reminded. Re-mine-ded."
>
> "Clarify," said Zulma's classmate Erick Diaz, 9, who began the year reading at a second-grade level. "When I come to a word I don't know, I look for chunks I do. Hailstones. Hail-stone-s."

The theory behind these deadening activities is that learning comprehension strategies will give students a shortcut to gaining greater expertise in reading. Supposedly, learning such strategies will quickly provide the skills they need to comprehend unfamiliar texts. But as the teachers in the school pointed out to the reporter, the methods did not seem to be working. Reading scores were not going up significantly. Perlstein reports that "staff members said they aren't sure what they might be doing wrong."

It is not the school staff that is responsible for what is going wrong in the school but the incorrect ideas that have been imposed on the staff — the formalistic theory behind these dull activities. That theory was succinctly stated by the superintendent of the district: "Once they learn the fundamentals of reading, writing, and math, they can pick up science and social studies on the double-quick," said [the] superintendent. "You're not going to be a scientist if you can't read."

The idea that reading skill is largely a set of general-purpose maneuvers that can be applied to any and all texts is one of the main barriers to our students' achievement in reading. It leads to activities that are deadening for agile and eager minds, and it carries big opportunity costs. These activities actually slow down the acquisition of true reading skill. They take up time that could be devoted to gaining general knowledge, which is the central requisite for high reading skill. The staff at the school Perlstein visited is dutifully wasting large amounts of valuable time by following the mistaken advice put forth by reading experts and by various "research-based" reading comprehension programs currently on offer. What these students and their teachers mainly need is a revolution in ideas.

IS SOCIETY TO BLAME?

The failure of romantic ideas to improve educational achievement is an inevitable result of their scientific inadequacy and inaccuracy. Reading is not, as romantics hold, either a natural acquisition or a formal skill. But mere scientific inadequacy can be a practical irrelevance in American education. Professors, including those who teach our teachers, do not easily give up their long-asserted ideas, even under the pressure of unfavorable scientific evidence. As Max Planck once memorably observed, new ideas take hold only when the old professors retire or die.[22] If the professors continue to think that romantic educational ideas are not scientifically wrong at all but quite correct, then they must find some other cause to explain why our students are not learning to read well. This alternative cause is American society — its distractions and its inequities. Under this theory, even students from advantaged circumstances do not learn to read well because of the distractions of modern culture — video games, computers, television, the movies. But that part of the theory is readily disposed of by pointing to developed countries whose students read better than ours yet spend as much or more time on video games, computers, television, and the movies.[23]

The more significant part of the blame-society theory is the claim that social conditions *necessarily* keep poor blacks and Hispanics from reading well. This is the theory of demographic determinism, which holds that reading problems have their roots outside school, in economic and cultural conditions (which is initially true). But the theory then goes on to claim (falsely) that low test scores in reading are beyond the power of schools by themselves to overcome. The familiar argument runs this way: since the schools can't remove poverty, it's unfair to suggest that they can bring everyone to proficiency in reading. It is poverty that causes low reading scores. Only after greater social justice is attained can we make real gains in those scores. The most eloquent defender of this view is Richard Rothstein, a former educational columnist for the *New York Times*. Rothstein argues that blaming the achievement gap mostly on failing schools is a mistake, because it diverts attention from the need to improve the economic and social gaps between children that thwart academic potential long before school starts.[24]

I completely concur with the desire to gain greater equality of social circumstance for all children. But that pressing social goal does not have to be used as a distraction from our schools' failure to make a dent in the reading achievement gap between demographic groups. It does no practical good to attack the economic status quo by defending the educational status quo. If schools by themselves can do a far better job of narrowing the achievement gap in reading, that will be a supreme contribution to the social aims that Rothstein and many others desire.

The proof that schools can narrow the gap is that some have in fact done so, both in this country and elsewhere, as we shall see. But until wider progress in narrowing the reading comprehension gap between social groups is achieved by many, many more American schools, demographic determinism will continue to seem plausible. It is nonetheless a flawed and dismal theory, which, while conveniently exculpating the schools, undermines the founding principle of democratic education. Rothstein and others who hold to the idea of demographic determinism might gladly abandon that view if our schools were able to make significant inroads into the current iron connection between reading scores and demographics. I will explain in this book how achievement in reading can be raised for all children and the test-score gap between social groups greatly narrowed at the same time.

MAKING BETTER IDEAS PREVAIL

This book makes strong arguments against currently dominant ideas. But its criticisms pertain to ideas, not persons. There is far too much criticism of teachers and principals for poor educational outcomes that have little to do with their native abilities or their desire to help children and a lot to do with prevailing educational ideas. To those who argue that the solution lies in hiring better teachers, I respond that much of the talk about low teacher quality is misplaced. If teachers now lack the knowledge they need to teach reading and other subjects well, it is not because they are innately incompetent but because they have been trained under faulty romantic ideas about the nature of reading and the worthlessness of "mere information." Nor are the education professors who trained them natively incompetent. They too have been trained under faulty romantic ideas.

When I say that current external conditions are adequate for making a big improvement in reading, I have in mind, for one thing, the classroom time now being allocated to the subject. States, districts, and schools are devoting plenty of time to it. Georgia and other states have mandated that 90 minutes each day shall be spent on reading in grades one through three. New York City and California have mandated 150 minutes. The state of Arizona suggests that schools may wish to spend 180 minutes a day on reading. Clearly these time allocations would be quite adequate to effect improvements if the classroom time were being well spent.

Just as the time currently spent on reading instruction is sufficient for real progress, so instructional materials for reading are also more than sufficient, at least in bulk, for sponsoring a big improvement in reading scores. Programs that cost publishers tens of millions of dollars to produce and schools hundreds of millions to buy are constantly being upgraded and revised. Young children carry home these weighty, expensive tomes filled with colored pictures. But the guiding ideas behind these programs are almost indistinguishable one from another.

Although the editors of several of these programs have strong credentials in education or psychology, the programs are far from up-to-date with regard to the relevant consensus in cognitive science. For instance, none of them fully reflects the current scientific consensus about the knowledge basis of reading. Cognitive scientists agree that reading comprehension requires prior "domain-specific" knowledge about the things that a text refers to, and that understanding the text consists of integrating this prior knowledge with the words in order to form a "situation model."[25] Constructing this mental situation model is what reading comprehension is. Existing reading programs, while they may pay lip service to this finding about the need for relevant background knowledge, fail systematically to exploit this fundamental insight into the nature of reading.

The reading problem can be solved if our schools begin to follow alternative ideas that stress the importance of a gradual acquisition of broad, enabling knowledge. One aim of this book is to help create a public demand for the kind of knowledge-oriented reading program that is needed. If that demand arises, then the rest can safely be left to the cunning of the market, for most of us in the United States desire the same democratic goal — to give all children an opportunity to succeed that depends mainly on their own talents and character and not on who their parents happen to be. A related aim of the book is to encourage an early curriculum that is oriented to knowledge rather than the will-o'-the-wisps of general, formal skills.

Thus my aims in this book are entirely constructive, despite the necessary criticisms I must make against inadequate ideas. They are also intensely practical. My call for a revolution in the teaching of subjects related to reading is issued in a period when activities in the elementary grades of the public schools are overshadowed by the provisions of the No Child Left Behind law (NCLB). Because of the exigencies of this law, the time could be ripe for making better ideas prevail.

Most citizens support the goals of NCLB, which was enacted with wide bipartisan support. One of its chief aims is to raise reading achievement and narrow the reading gap between demographic groups. But support for the law has begun to diminish, because it has proved immensely difficult for the schools to fulfill its key requirement that all demographic groups must make "adequate yearly progress" for the schools to qualify for a large annual sum from the federal government — a share of some $12 billion. Since many schools have found it nearly impossible to show adequate yearly progress in reading for all groups, even when subjects like history and science are being neglected to spend more time on reading, there has been an outcry against the act, and also against the yearly tests that measure progress. The U.S. Department of Education has been compelled to soften its requirements.

No situation better illustrates the importance of theories in education than this practical impasse. The legislation was enacted on the theory that if many children are being left behind in reading and if there is a large reading gap between demographic groups, the schools must not be concentrating their efforts properly on those needy children; hence we will build into the act incentives that will induce the schools to focus their efforts more equitably, so that these children will begin to catch up. Note that this theory assumes that the education world actually knows how to improve reading scores for all groups and that incentives must be applied because the schools are simply not putting forth the effort needed to help low-income and minority children.

Since no school wants to be labeled inadequate, the law's provisions have had a tremendous impact on the public schools, well documented in Linda Perlstein's description of the Highland Elementary School in Maryland. Like that school, most schools seem to be trying as hard as they can. They were already instituting many of the reforms that are called for, even before the official provisions of NCLB began to fall due. That is, they have called in outside experts; they have used new curricula in the form of intensive reading programs; they have decreased management authority at the school level, and some districts have entered into contracts with private companies to operate schools that are not making annual yearly progress.

With all this intensive NCLB activity, we might expect a significant change in reading achievement, and gains have indeed been made in the earliest grades, when sounding out (rather than comprehension) is chiefly being tested. But schools are currently having great difficulty meeting annual-yearly-progress requirements, and it is unlikely that we will begin to see significant reading improvement in the next year or so, except for improvements in the teaching of sounding out — of phonics. But the credit for *that* improvement should go to the heroes of the systematic phonics movement, who through their efforts have now brought effective teaching of decoding into many reading programs. This improvement was due to a change of ideas, not to a system of incentives in the new law. The schools are trying very hard, without much success. For them to make real improvements in reading comprehension similar to the improvements in sounding out, they will need better ideas.

By no means should these observations be taken as fundamental criticisms of NCLB and its important aims, which are the same as the aims of this book. It is the most hopeful and important federal education legislation that has been enacted in recent years. The legislators who passed the law can hardly be faulted for assuming that American educational experts possess enough scientific and practical knowledge to attain the goals of the act, so long as the act offered sufficient carrots and sticks. They were right about the inducements. They were wrong about the experts.

The dominant ideas in American education are virtually unchallenged within the educational community. American educational expertise (which is not the same as educational expertise in nations that perform better than we do) has a monolithic character in which dissent is stifled. This is because of the history of American education schools. As Geraldine Clifford, James Guthrie, Diane Ravitch, and others have shown, the history of these schools, which are institutions that train almost all of the teachers and administrators who must carry out the provisions of NCLB, is the history of intellectual cloning.[26] At the beginning of the twentieth century, the parent organism, Teachers College at Columbia University, exported professors and the romantic principles we have discussed, resulting in an intellectual sameness across the nation's education schools. Even today criticism of those fundamental ideas is hard to find in these institutions.

The fate of NCLB and of academic improvement will be decided in the sphere of ideas. American ed school ideas march under the banner of continual reform, but the reform, given different names in different eras, is always the same one, being carried out against the same enemy. The enemy is dull, soulless drill and the stuffing of children's minds with dead, inert information. These are to be replaced by natural, engaging activities (naturalism). A lot of dead information is to be replaced by all-purpose, how-to knowledge (formalism). These are the two perennial ideas of the American educational world. These two principles together constitute a kind of theology that is drilled into prospective teachers like a catechism.

In practice the two principles are not always consistent with each other. As we saw in Ms. Witthaus's class, an adherence to the formalistic idea — the how-to notion of reading comprehension that stresses clarifying, summarizing, questioning — will inevitably lead to drill-like activities, which will be anathematized by the naturalistic principle that learning should be an engaging activity. This inherent conflict leads in turn to resentment of the idea that the children should be constantly tested, since the new accountability provisions of the law, it is thought, have forced schools to engage in all of this soul-killing drill in clarifying and summarizing. That naturalism and formalism should inevitably be in conflict doesn't, however, mean that either is to be given up as part of the theology that is taught to teachers in our ed schools. The internal conflict between the principles simply generates the need for continual reform, and offers an enemy that is always to be resisted, even when it has been generated by the drills that go with formalistic ideas.

The dominant principles of naturalism and formalism, being opposed to the systematic teaching of a great deal of information, are deadly enemies of the reading goals of NCLB. Advances in reading will depend on students gaining a great deal of information. This conflict of ideas is, then, the root cause of the impasse between the NCLB law and the schools, for the only way to improve scores in reading comprehension and to narrow the reading gap between groups is systematically to provide children with the wide-ranging, specific background knowledge they need to comprehend what they read.

Old people grow blunt; they haven't time for slow niceties. Let me be blunt about the implications of the intellectual history I have traced in this chapter and the implications of this book. If its recommendations are followed, reading scores will rise for all groups of children, and so will scores in math and science, because, as common sense would predict, reading is strongly correlated with ability to learn in all subjects. Equally important, social justice will be served, because the reading gap between social groups will be greatly narrowed by following the book's pro-knowledge recommendations. If you are a teacher, the book's suggestions will help your children. If you are a parent, they will help your child. The book will describe how instructional time can be used most productively, how language and vocabulary growth can be fostered most effectively, and how the knowledge that is most enabling for reading comprehension can be made an integral part of a child's reading program. If such reading programs were widely used in conjunction with a coherent, knowledge-based curriculum, then reading scores would rise significantly across the nation and across social groups. That would finally defeat the dragon of demographic determinism. It would bring us closer to the ideal of giving all children an opportunity to succeed that depends on their own talents and character rather than on who their parents happen to be. It would make the American future brighter.

2
SOUNDING OUT: JUST THE BEGINNING OF READING

WHAT WE'VE RECENTLY ACHIEVED

RECENTLY SCHOOLS HAVE BEGUN to do a much better job of teaching all children to become good first-step readers who can turn printed symbols into sounds and words quickly and accurately, a process called decoding. No one should underestimate the huge importance of this advance, as compared with the very uncertain results that our schools were achieving in teaching decoding just a decade ago. Before I correct four prevalent misconceptions about reading, I would like to pay homage to those who helped win this immensely important battle. In that effort there have been real heroes. First-rate scientists like Marilyn Jager Adams and Jeanne Chall, whose pathbreaking book, *Learning to Read: The Great Debate* (1965), began the decades-long change, encouraged by the farsighted government administrator Reid Lyon and by the crusading editor of *The American Educator,* Elizabeth McPike, have turned the tide against the romantic notion that decoding is best regarded as a natural process, in the same way children learn to speak.[1] Such an approach is a thoroughly incorrect idea that has in the past left many children by the wayside, unable to sound out words rapidly and accurately. These researchers have shown that the best and fastest way to teach decoding is through persistent, explicit instruction, a little at a time, starting no later than kindergarten. The research consensus on this conclusion is strong, and empirical evidence supporting it is voluminous.[2]

To have brought our romantically inclined schools to such an unromantic view of early reading has taken more than research and dissemination; it has taken other kinds of heroes in the struggle of ideas — activists like Marion Joseph, the smart California grandmother who saw that there was something wrong with the way her grandchild was (or wasn't) learning how to sound out words. Marion Joseph has been credited with turning the entire school system of California (and the publishers who sell books to California) toward the systematic and explicit teaching of the alphabetic/phonemic system of written English.[3] The resulting improvements in first-step reading are already apparent, not only in California but across the country. Because of these intellectual and policy advances during the past decade, more and more of our children are becoming skilled decoders.

But becoming a skilled decoder does not insure that one will become a skilled reader. It used to be thought that once students were able to decode words fluently and accurately, skilled comprehension would follow automatically, through practice and broad reading. As with most widely held beliefs, there is some truth to this idea. A small number of children, especially those of well-educated parents, are able to become proficient readers simply by growing up in a rich oral-language environment and then reading widely to gain general knowledge. But since fewer than half our students actually reach proficiency in reading comprehension, the present reality has not conformed to the old assumption that good comprehension follows automatically from gaining a good early start in decoding.

In retrospect, we can see why there was a flaw in this idea. After mastering decoding, a student who reads widely can indeed, under the right circumstances, gain greater knowledge and thence better reading comprehension. But such gains will occur only if the student already knows enough to comprehend the meaning of what he or she is decoding! Many specialists estimate that a child or an adult needs to understand around 90 percent of the words in a passage in order to learn to understand the other 10 percent of the words.[4] Moreover, it's not just the words that the student has to grasp the meaning of; it's also the kind of reality that the words are referring to.[5] When a child doesn't understand those word meanings and those referred-to realities, being good at sounding out words is a dead end. Reading becomes a kind of Catch-22.

In other words, in order to learn how to read with understanding, you already have to be able to read with understanding. Long before Joseph Heller's *Catch-22*, his idea was implied in the Gospel of Matthew, which stated that those who already have shall gain more, while from those who have not shall be taken away even what they have. Alluding to this biblical passage, reading researchers have spoken of the "Matthew effect" in reading. Those who already have good language understanding will gain still more language proficiency, while those who lack initial understanding will fall further and further behind.[6] The new frontier in literacy will need to build on this insight. Schooling will need to pay close and systematic attention to the concrete knowledge that all students are gradually acquiring, so that each early gain will lead to later ones. This will not only raise general academic achievement in reading and other subjects, it will also narrow the large academic achievement gap between haves and have-nots. But to accomplish this great goal, we will need a new generation of heroes like Jeanne Chall and Marion Joseph to conduct the next phase of the battle, which is to make sure that our students become skilled comprehenders of what they read and hear.

The change in the teaching of reading that this book proposes can be carried out only if we clear away some widespread conceptual underbrush. We need to see the reading comprehension problem for what it primarily is — a knowledge problem. Once children learn how to decode the printed word accurately and fluently, the main reason they do not read as well as they should is that they do not know as much as they should about the various things the printed words refer to. And our children will not learn those enabling things unless they are given the opportunity to learn them, an opportunity currently denied them because reading is misconceived as a special, separate skill that, once learned, will grow automatically and be transferred from one text to another.

Is Reading Like Listening?

When we think of children learning to read, we usually visualize their gradual "development" from laborious sounding out of the letters ("cuh-a-tuh") to a fast and accurate pronunciation of the word ("cat") and on to a fast and accurate pronunciation of whole sentences and paragraphs ("The cat in the hat is on the mat"). Up to this point, the standard picture is basically right. But the further extension of the development idea is not. It is usually thought that the progress of reading skill continues to follow a steady "growth" from *The Cat in the Hat* to *The Mill on the Floss.* Behind that notion is an implicit sense that reading is an activity that follows its own separate course of growth, which is different from talking and listening. The superficial differences between writing and talking must not mislead us into making a fundamental distinction between oral and written speech. The stakes are high in avoiding this mistake, because as long as we incorrectly view progress in reading as something separate from general progress in language and knowledge, we parents and teachers will continue to fail to foster our children's progress in reading and general intellectual achievement.

The crucial years for gaining a good start in language are the early years.[7] In recent decades, since reading has been misconceived as a separate skill, there has been a relative neglect of enhancing oral language in the early years of schooling (ages four through seven). All across America, such neglect has proved fateful for children's reading in later years. Great opportunities are being squandered. A good early start in verbal knowledge and world knowledge leads children to accrue still more knowledge each subsequent year, as in an interest-bearing bank account. At the youngest ages, two through seven, long before children can read as well as they can listen, progress in language occurs chiefly through listening and talking, not through reading and writing. But because we have thought of reading and writing as separate from listening and talking, we have tended to spend large amounts of time — too much time — on the simple cat-in-the-hat kinds of written material that young children are able to read and understand for themselves. We have failed to focus effectively on the knowledge of both language and the world that children can gain in those years only through speaking and listening, not through reading.

In grades one and two, self-reading materials ("See Spot run!") must necessarily be extremely simple. Not only must the texts be made up of words that are easy for the child to decode, they must also be very limited in conceptual demands, for the child's laborious process of turning the printed marks into words and sentences is so taxing that he or she has little attention left for understanding anything but simple ideas. But this often trivial material is far below the comprehension potential of young children from all walks of life. If we do not spend large amounts of time reading aloud and discussing challenging material with children — material that is well beyond their ability to decode with understanding — we miss a critical opportunity to increase their knowledge of language and of the world — the kind of knowledge that will prove decisive for reading in later years. Because current language programs incorrectly view reading and oral speech as separate developmental processes, they spend little time in coherent knowledge and language enhancement. This missed opportunity is particularly fateful for disadvantaged children, who are already far behind their advantaged classmates in general and verbal knowledge.[8]

In past decades, the idea that reading and listening are separate spheres was a subject of scientific inquiry. It was claimed that expert readers process the written word through a speedy, separate process that short-circuits the time-consuming activity of sounding out words. We now know that this theory is incorrect. The way we process the written word and the way we process the spoken word are essentially the same. Readers must go through what researchers call "the phonological loop," which informs our reading and speaking as well as our thinking.[9]

Once the issue of written and spoken language is brought under the glare of thoughtful examination, few people would openly defend the idea that progress in reading and in language comprehension are separate. It is intuitively obvious that any limit on children's ability to understand a text that is being read aloud to them usually limits their ability to understand that same text when they read it by themselves. Yet this obvious connection has not been adequately exploited in early reading materials and programs, which take such a formalistic view of reading comprehension that they neglect the systematic expansion of children's general knowledge and accompanying vocabulary. The systematic phonics in these programs (now, on the whole, admirable) are not backed up by a systematic approach to the background knowledge that children will need for later reading comprehension.

Many assume that gains in "developing" reading comprehension must wait upon gains in developing the child's fluency and accuracy at decoding, as though the two phases were part of a single developmental process called reading. They assume that if learning to decode print is arduous, then learning to understand it must be similarly difficult, which gives rise to the idea that comprehending a printed text is something special, hard, and artificial, requiring special kinds of "strategies." But we have known since 1974 (thanks to the work of Thomas Sticht) that listening ability in grade two reliably forecasts reading ability in grade five.[10] This empirical work confirms that reading skill is correlated with listening skill — or, to put the case more accurately, proficient reading and proficient listening both depend on an ability to comprehend language, quite apart from whether the language is expressed orally or in writing. The assumption that an advance in comprehension must wait on an advance in decoding fluency is, bluntly, wrong. Every gain in oral speech, in knowledge and in vocabulary and in the conventions of formal discourse, that children make in kindergarten or first grade is ultimately a gain in reading comprehension, whether or not that fact is immediately evident. If children's progress in language and knowledge is held hostage to their progress in decoding, their ability to read with comprehension will be unnecessarily retarded. If children are brought to speak and understand speech well in the early years, their reading future is bright.[11]

It is precisely for the sake of reading and writing that we need to place a great deal of emphasis in the early grades on nonwritten, oral activities — on adults reading aloud coherent and challenging material, on discussing it, on having children elaborate on these materials. I say "elaborate" because it is essential for young children to become familiar with the more public genres of oral speech, which are the main genres of reading and writing. We need to avoid potential confusion on this score. While the ability to understand language, whether written or spoken, is an underlying ability required for reading, and while language is the underlying reality in both cases, there are some practical differences between conversational language, which is usually informal in nature, and written language, which has to be elaborated.

The nearest example is our everyday experience of radio and television. A person can read written marks out loud over radio or television, and millions of listeners, some of whom cannot themselves read, can understand what that person is saying. Radio and television are like reading aloud to a large, diverse audience. If we examine the differences between radio speech and ordinary talk, we begin to see what children need to be taught about the special formal conventions of reading and writing in order to become good readers and writers.

Radio talk and writing have the same task to perform. Both are addressed to an unknown, unseen audience. The speaker or writer must know how to do this in order to be understood, and the listener or reader must know the background knowledge that the speaker or writer is taking for granted. Both sides are parties to an elaborate system of conventions that have been accrued over many years — namely, how to speak to strangers. Before coming to school, the young child has already learned how to speak and listen to intimates — to parents and caregivers and to peers. In those kinds of exchanges, he or she can take a great deal for granted and does not have to be formal and explicit in language. Going out into the wider world, though, the child has to learn this new use of language. Children when they first come to school have not usually learned how to make themselves understood to unseen strangers. Learning how to read and write is very much tied up with learning how to listen and speak to strangers.[12]

Here's an example of radio talk, taken at random from an interview on *Morning Edition* on National Public Radio. The oral speech that takes place over the radio is so similar to written speech that it can be transcribed directly to make plausible sense in writing.[13]

STEVE INSKEEP (host): What may have been the best weekend of tennis in years ended yesterday. Roger Federer won his second straight Wimbledon men's singles title. The day before, Maria Sharapova won the women's title. The teenager stunned the two-time defending champion, Serena Williams. Commentator John Feinstein joins us now. Good morning, John.

JOHN FEINSTEIN: Good morning, Steve.

INSKEEP: So Federer beat Andy Roddick in four sets. Is it fair to say they brought out the best in each other?

FEINSTEIN: It was the best men's tennis match I've seen in a long -

time, certainly at Wimbledon, where serve-and-volley is so dominant when the men play. There was a lot of play from the back court. The match went back and forth in terms of who was in control. It looked as if Roddick was going to take command just before there was the inevitable rain delay in the third set, and then Federer stormed back to take over again. And I thought the whole thing was great, including the fact that at the end of the match, Roddick went around the net to hug Federer and congratulate him. It just smacked of everything that's good in tennis, and it's been so long since we've seen that sort of thing, I actually found it encouraging, and I haven't been encouraged about the sport for a long time.

INSKEEP: Makings of a friendly rivalry there?

FEINSTEIN: That's what you would hope. The problem is, as Roddick noted after the match, Federer has dominated him. He's beaten him six times out of seven now, but Roddick showed that he isn't just the serve-and-volleyer yesterday, that he has more game than that. And with Pete Sampras gone and Andre Agassi about to go from the sport, these are the guys who have to be the rivalry. Tennis is such an individual game, you need rivalries, like Connors and McEnroe and Borg and McEnroe and Evert and Navratilova. And these guys have the potential to be that on the men's side, yes.

This conversation makes perfect sense as a piece of writing, because it does just what writing has to do — it addresses itself to strangers. This kind of explicit, formal talk is indeed different from the kinds of ordinary conversation that children and adults engage in. As a parent or teacher, we can help our children grasp what reading and writing are like by practicing pretend radio or other audience-directed speeches. In the classroom, the teacher can and should ask children frequently to make formal prepared and unprepared presentations to the class. This is the best practice for becoming a good writer and reader that we can devise for young children, because it enacts the communicative situation of reading and writing without involving the arduous process of learning to sound out and form letters accurately and fluently. That decoding task is absolutely essential, but as we've seen, it is a different task, and it is a long-range one that should not hold back progress in language and knowledge.

Not only children exhibit the difference between formal speech and ordinary conversation. The distinction is an essential feature of learning to function in a speech community. Real conversations are often incomprehensible to listeners who happen to be unaware of the specific context in which the conversation occurs. This was very evident in the famous Nixon tapes, in which actual conversations were secretly tape-recorded and then transcribed. Here is a random sample.[14]

PRESIDENT: I suggest that we sit over here, everybody. More room and, uh — [coughing] Sit down.

UNIDENTIFIED: Yeah, this —

UNIDENTIFIED: But —

UNIDENTIFIED: Oh, that's all right.

UNIDENTIFIED: I had that senator [unintelligible]

UNIDENTIFIED: Came in and got me nervous, uh, he —

UNIDENTIFIED: If he'll go with you, well, that's great.

UNIDENTIFIED: Very clever.

UNIDENTIFIED: Phil, uh, [unintelligible]

PRESIDENT: They're counting on Hubert.

UNIDENTIFIED: Concentrate on Hubert.

PRESIDENT: Hubert is supposed to have told Meany that I, uh —

SHULTZ: I don't know that you've met Don Rice, from the Office of Management and Budget.

PRESIDENT: Yes.

SHULTZ: Don Rice. [Several (unintelligible) voices]

RICE: How are you?

SHULTZ: I talked with Meany this afternoon about the SST.

PRESIDENT: What'd he say?

SHULTZ: He said he was all out on it. If there was anything we wanted him to do, he wanted to do it. He'd be ready to do it. They —

PRESIDENT: Well, could you ask him to, could you ask him, could you phone him back after this meeting and ask him to call Hubert Humphrey, with the understanding he, uh —

SHULTZ: Yeah.

Presumably this excerpt made coherent sense to the participants. The transcript makes little coherent sense as a piece of writing, though, because it is not consciously addressed to others, as if they were radio listeners or readers who are unaware of the immediate physical and situational context. Early reading programs in the schools have paid too little attention to instruction in the special conventions and obligations that must constrain speakers and listeners in public situations.

Reading comprehension is not a technical skill that must be learned as though the text were a given that drifted down from the sky. It is the other side of knowing how to speak and write in an understandable way to strangers within a particular speech community. The skills of reading and writing, like the skills of speaking and listening, are infused with the traditions of a particular group. The perfection of written communication by means of a clear prose style took quite a long time. In English it took two centuries, from 1500 to 1700.[15] But while writing and printing led over time to the refinement of ever more efficient rhetorical techniques, these are fundamentally the same techniques that people have always adopted when they are speaking to large, heterogeneous groups. There is no special characteristic of speech that makes reading and writing inherently different from listening and speaking.

The transcripts of radio speech and ordinary conversation are not merely incidental to this point. They illustrate something quite fundamental about reading and writing — that what counts is not whether the speech is recorded in print or via computer, encoded in radio waves, or produced as vibrations of air molecules from mouth to ear. Psychologically, all of these must pass through the "phono-logical loop." What counts most from the standpoint of language comprehension is the kind of utterance that is being engaged in and whether the audience has the background knowledge, including knowledge of speech conventions, they need to comprehend it. To understand the transcript of Steve Inskeep and John Feinman, you don't need special skills unique to reading; you need to know some-thing about the tennis scene.

Effective speech on radio and TV, whether monologue, dialogue, or drama, always clues in the listener to what is needed to make the speech comprehensible ("What may have been the best weekend of tennis in years ended yesterday. Roger Federer won his second straight Wimbledon men's singles title"). Radio talk transcribed into writing is easy to understand because it gives explicit clues in pre-cisely the way writing must to be understood. Children need to learn that when they have to address a big, heterogeneous audience, such as a classroom full of peers, they have to be more explicit both in syntax and in overtly stated background knowledge.[16] They also need to build their vocabularies and gradually gain a sense of what others in their speech community take for granted. They need to learn these things to be effective speakers and listeners as well as good readers.

In view of the inseparability of oral and written speech, ne-glecting intensive formal oral language enhancement during the long hours devoted to reading in the early grades has been more than a missed opportunity; it has been a disaster for social justice. Early oral language enhancement plus the systematic teaching of enabling knowledge are the keys to later gains in all academic areas, and also to narrowing the achievement gap between demographic groups. It is in early language learning that the Matthew effect begins to take hold. Those who know many words and who possess the background knowledge to comprehend what they mean will learn more words and world knowledge later on, while those who know few words in early grades fall further and further behind in later grades. There is every scientific reason to predict that an intensive and well-focused effort to enhance language and knowledge during the classroom reading period in early grades will not only raise reading achievement for all students, it will help narrow the gap between social groups.

FILLING IN THE BLANKS

Two mothers are discussing their very precocious kindergartners: "Can your child read?" "Oh, yes. She was reading at age three."

A great start for that child! But we can be sure that the precocious youngster was not reading Kant's *Critique of Pure Reason*, or, for that matter, the local newspaper. *Reading* in common use has tended to combine both senses of the word — the decoding of printed marks into the sounds of language, which is mainly what the proud mother is referring to, and subsequently the understanding of what the decoded language means. The combined meaning is a perfectly useful shortcut that is appropriate for those who normally understand what they are reading. It makes good sense to ask an adult friend, "Have you read *Pride and Prejudice*?" assuming that if she has read the book, she has more or less understood it.

But this vague combining of decoding and comprehension has caused confusion. It leads people to think that if they can just get children to pronounce the words fluently and to understand simple texts, then, in the normal developmental course of things, these skills will gradually increase and will be successfully applied to more advanced texts. Yet we observe from low national reading scores that decoding fluency in grade four, when our children's scores are moderately high by international standards, does *not* automatically develop into comprehension fluency in grade twelve, when our students' scores are low.[17]

It has been assumed that just as you can transfer general decoding skill to all texts, you can similarly transfer a general ability to understand the words that have been decoded. It is true that given a good start in decoding, a child will develop fluency and accuracy in decoding with practice. And it is also true that decoding is a skill that can be transferred from one text to another. But the progress of a child's reading comprehension is different. That progress does not follow a reliable course of development. Comprehension is not a skill that automatically grows into an ability to cope with complex materials once a child has been given a start with simple ones.

The confusion may have arisen because there does indeed exist such a thing as general reading skill — a general ability to understand a wide diversity of texts. This is, of course, the educational goal for children that we are striving for. As we will see, general reading skill applies only to texts that are consciously directed to a general audience within a definite speech community. Even a well-educated person is not expected to understand a technical text on astrophysics or computer science. Within that limitation, well-educated people can and do exhibit a general proficiency in reading comprehension, and we can indeed reliably measure that proficiency on reading tests, just as the test-makers claim. If children score well on those tests, they can read well. It means they have good general reading ability.

But a look at those standardized reading tests will disclose that they always include a diversity of passages on quite different subjects — a feature that is absolutely critical to their validity and reliability as tests. If they sampled just one kind of subject matter, they would prove to be inaccurate as measures of general reading ability. Someone who reads well about the Civil War may not necessarily read well about molecular interactions. If we want to measure *general* reading ability on a test, we must include passages that sample a person's *general knowledge* of several kinds of subjects. Test-makers found this out by experimentation and common sense long before cognitive science demonstrated that what counts in understanding a text (once it has been verbally decoded) is not, as is supposed in current reading programs, a general working vocabulary plus some comprehension strategies. General reading comprehension ability is much more than comprehension strategies; it requires a definite range of general knowledge.

One elegant experiment was conducted to find out how important domain-specific knowledge is in actual reading tasks.[18] It tested how well students who had generally high technical skills in decoding and comprehension strategies performed in comparison to students with generally low technical reading skills but prior knowledge of the subject matter of the text. In two of the four groups studied, one had good decoding skills but poor knowledge of the subject, baseball, while the poor-decoding group knew a lot about baseball. As predicted, the reading comprehension of the low-skills, baseball-knowing group proved superior to the reading comprehension of the high-skills, baseball-ignorant group for that particular text. These results have been replicated in other situations and knowledge domains and show the powerful effect of prior knowledge on actual reading skill.[19]

As scientists have probed more deeply into the nature of language comprehension, this kind of result has proved less and less surprising. Researchers have discovered that what the text implies but doesn't say is a necessary part of its understood meaning. In fact, what the text *doesn't* say often far exceeds what it says. The reader or listener has to fill in the blanks and make the unstated connections in order to make sense of the text. This is hardly a new observation. The ancient Greeks knew it, and Aristotle even gave the phenomenon a name — enthymeme, which is technically a syllogism with some of the logically necessary steps left out.[20] For instance, if I say, "All men are mortal, so Socrates is mortal," everyone will understand what I say. But that is because their relevant knowledge enables them to supply the missing inference: "Socrates is a man." Comprehension skill cannot be automatically transferred from one text to another, because the skill of comprehension is basically the skill of filling in enough of what has been left unsaid — that is, filling in enough blanks — to make sense of the text. The ability to fill in these blanks depends entirely on whether children know what is to be filled in.

To different extents, all speech has these blank spaces. The more a speaker can take for granted, the less he has to say explicitly and the more rapid and concentrated communication can become. Speed is important, because a person can keep in mind only a very few items at a time, which means that richness of meaning is gained by condensing ordinary oral speech. Written speech is the same, only less so. It leaves less unspoken. It is more explicit, because writers know that they must make it so in order to be understood. But writing always leaves a great deal unsaid.

Cognitive psychologists have determined that when a text is being understood, the reader (or listener) is filling in a lot of the unstated connections between the words to create an imagined situation model based on domain-specific knowledge.[21] This constructed situation model constitutes the understood meaning of the text. Take, for example, this passage from my book *What Your Second Grader Needs to Know:*

> In 1861, the Civil War started. It lasted until 1865. It was American against American, North against South. The Southerners called Northerners "Yankees." Northerners called Southerners "Rebels," or "Rebs" for short. General Robert E. Lee was in charge of the Southern army. General Ulysses S. Grant was in charge of the Northern army. They were very different men. General Lee was a tall, dignified gentleman. General Grant was scruffy-looking, and to tell the truth, he drank too much. Both men were brilliant military leaders.

Potentially, this passage is usefully informative to a second-grader — but only if he or she understands it. Take the phrase "North against South." A wealth of preexisting background information is needed to understand that simple phrase — going far beyond the root idea of compass directions, which is simply the necessary first step. The child needs a general idea of the geography of the United States and needs to infer that the named compass directions stand for geographical regions. Then a further inference or construction is needed: the child has to understand that the names of geographical regions stand for the populations of those regions and that those populations have been organized into some sort of collectivity so they can raise armies. That's just an initial stab at unpacking what the child must infer to understand the phrase "North against South." A full, explicit account of the taken-for-granted knowledge that someone would need to construct a situation model from all of this passage would take many pages of analysis.

To understand language, whether spoken or written, we need to construct a situation model consisting of meanings construed from the explicit words of the text as well as meanings inferred or constructed from relevant background knowledge. The spoken and the unspoken taken together constitute the meaning. Without this relevant, unspoken background knowledge, we can't understand the text.

That is why we are able to understand some texts but not others, no matter how well we can decode the words. We possess the relevant knowledge in some cases, and in those cases we can understand what we are reading, but we lack it in others, and in those cases we cannot comprehend the text. Since relevant, domain-specific knowledge is an absolute requirement for reading comprehension, there is no way around the need for children to gain broad general knowledge in order to gain broad general proficiency in reading.

ARE SOME KINDS OF KNOWLEDGE BETTER THAN OTHERS?

According to received views in the American educational community, no specific background knowledge is needed for reading. *Any* general background knowledge will serve. This innocent-sounding idea, so liberating to the teacher and the student, frees the American school from any requirement to teach a specific body of knowledge. This supposed liberation from "mere" information and rote learning is one of the most precious principles of American educational thought, and lies at its very core. Its proponents disparage those who favor a definite, cumulative course of study for children as "traditional," "hidebound," and "reactionary," to mention only the more polite terms.

Yet the supposedly liberating and humane idea that any general background knowledge will serve to educate children and make them proficient readers is not only incorrect, it is also very old and tired; it has had its day for at least half a century, during which time, as we've seen, American reading proficiency and verbal SAT scores have declined drastically.[22] Scapegoats for the decline, such as television and social forces, have been invoked to explain it, but they cannot fully explain why other nations, equally addicted to television but not to American educational theories that disparage "mere" information, have not suffered a similarly drastic decline in reading proficiency.[23]

To see how that misconception has persisted, note the response of the educational community to the now well-accepted finding in research that reading proficiency requires background knowledge. A typical response says, "Of course knowledge is needed. Therefore we should teach reading on the basis of each individual child's already existing world knowledge. Children come from different backgrounds. The child constructs meaning from the text starting with his or her already existing background knowledge. The goal of reading instruction is primarily to make the child ever more fluent in using comprehension strategies to ferret out meaning." A statement on background knowledge from the famous Bank Street School of Education in New York City is characteristic:[24]

Background Knowledge

All readers bring to the reading/writing process their own growing knowledge of language, the world, and their understandings of how print is used to convey meaning. A child who is often read to, or who regularly sees adults reading and writing for personal tasks and pleasure, will expect that reading and writing play useful roles in life and are valued activities. A child who has limited exposure to reading and writing will have very different expectations and understandings. Each of these situations, however, provides some of the background knowledge that children bring to the act of reading and writing.

Effective teaching fosters these expectations of reading and writing as purposeful and meaningful acts, and honors and builds on learners' diverse areas of knowledge through thoughtful selection of reading materials and activities. For example, a child interested in and knowledgeable about dinosaurs will be well equipped to explore a new book about these prehistoric creatures. Another child who is less familiar with dinosaurs may be equally intrigued by the same book, but will benefit from some preliminary introduction to the content. For example, before reading, the child might spend time looking at a variety of pictures of dinosaurs — skeletons as well as "life-like" images, or talking about when they existed, or what they ate . . .

Beginning readers, too, need to learn to use their own background knowledge. Helping them activate and extend this knowledge and selecting texts that build on what they already know or understand about their world support their attempts to make sense of what they are reading.

This is a good summary of the doctrines taught to teachers by schools of education across the nation. Academic skills should be built up from the knowledge that the child already has as well as from the knowledge that is most interesting and appropriate to the child. It is highly inconvenient to this doctrine that research has shown a body of specific background knowledge to be necessary for reading proficiency and therefore it should be taught in school. This runs up against the dominant view that the content of schooling should be left up entirely to the individual locality, the individual teacher, or the needs of the individual student and that the content of schooling is in itself far less important than the learning of formal skills such as "reading" and "critical thinking."

As with most American educational doctrines, the notion that we must start with the child's individual knowledge has some validity. The background knowledge that a child brings to bear in trying to comprehend a text obviously *has* to be the knowledge she has already acquired before beginning to read. The important question is whether a reading program should leave the matter there, given the fact that many children lack the general background knowledge they need to understand a diversity of writings. How current programs, fragmented and trivial in content, could effectively provide the general knowledge that children require in order to gain proficiency in reading is not explained by proponents of the status quo. Rather, as the passage quoted above indicates, the status quo asserts that any reasonably diverse set of readings will, by its very diversity, supply the kinds of knowledge and experiences children need.

The alert reader will notice that a vague, unspecific concept of the content called for in a reading program masks what is ultimately a formalistic conception of reading. The status quo asserts that offering students different kinds of writings will automatically prepare them to read different kinds of texts, whether or not the chosen selections are designed to foster the specific knowledge that is most enabling for future reading. The practical result is that early reading programs offer the child a fragmented series of readings with little sustained information or coherence.

This is a tragic sin of omission. I believe that this indifference to specific, cumulative subject matter, more than any other single trait of reading programs, has prevented them from significantly improving reading comprehension. The reason that the content-indifferent theory has not worked out in practice is that it is thoroughly inadequate as a theory. For many years now, as we've seen, cognitive science has rejected a formalistic conception of language comprehension. Its findings are exacting. We now know that the relevant background knowledge needed for reading comprehension must be domain-specific in order to enable the reader to form an adequate situation model.[25] The finding that verbal comprehension consists of forming a situation model is a powerful and clarifying idea that is the fruit of a half-century of work in psycholinguistics.[26]

Let's take another example against formalism. Schoolchildren all over the nation recite the Pledge of Allegiance, and gradually many of them begin to understand it. When they do, they construct an accurate situation model from the words. They understand that, along with their fellow students, they are engaged in making a promise. Setting aside the fact that it takes children quite a while to figure out what "allegiance" is, let's consider the flag. If the flag isn't physically present during the pledge, the children need to know what it is and what it looks like. They need to know what a nation is and that nations have flags. It is not stated in the pledge that other nations have their flags, just as we have ours, but that unstated notion is an essential part of the understood situation, which entails that we are loyal to *our* flag, which is not everybody's flag. Other unstated things must be understood as part of the situation, such as the notion of a solemn contract, which, once made, cannot morally be broken. All of these things are part of the situation model that the children must construct for themselves to understand the pledge, and because these things are unstated, they must construct the situation model from relevant knowledge that they already have. Without that specific background knowledge, they cannot understand the pledge. General, unspecified background knowledge won't do.

If formalistic theories of reading were actually true, it would be a great convenience for everyone. Controversy could be avoided and reading scores would rise. No one would have to make hard decisions about what to teach and what order it should be taught in. Deciding on a specific sequence of content is a difficult intellectual issue even for those who have misgivings about formalism in reading. The contents of education in a democracy are always proper subjects for debate. But the debate will be more productive if its participants understand that certain subjects are essential by virtue of their inherent necessity for communication through speech and writing.

This enabling shared knowledge ought to be kept safe from ideological and political controversy, for if there is indeed knowledge that all children must have if they are to become proficient readers in our speech community, then it is our duty to determine what that knowledge is and show why it is needed. Only such a fully open approach is likely to solve the political as well as the intellectual difficulties of admitting that reading is a content-ridden skill. The solution to the problem of determining these contents lies not just in cognitive science but in history. An ever-changing shared history determines what the enabling, shared knowledge is for any society.

In speaking to other Americans, I cannot make everything explicit. I cannot continually define the meanings of words (for then I would need to define the words of the definition, and so on); nor can I fully define the situations to which the words refer, since that would in turn require still further explanations of still further situations. When I say, "Johnny, go fetch the wheelbarrow," I have to assume that Johnny already knows what and where the wheelbarrow is. If I begin a document with the words, "We the people of the United States, in order to form a more perfect Union," the knowledge I take for granted is extensive. Indeed, one of Chief Justice John Marshall's famous comments about the U.S. Constitution was that "to contain an accurate detail of all the subdivisions of which its great powers will admit, and all the means by which they may be carried into execution, would partake of the prolixity of a legal code and could scarcely be embraced by the human mind."[27]

The knowledge that speech and writing takes for granted is recognized by the language community as something that can in fact be taken for granted. To assure communication when I address a stranger, I have to estimate what I can assume and what I must explain. Hence, my knowledge of what I can take for granted in communicating with strangers is critical to my successful membership in a speech community.[28] As part of my general speech competence, therefore, I must share with others a sense of what can be taken for granted, and this sense is also part of my reading and writing ability. This shared, assumed knowledge is something our children must learn if they are to become competent readers and writers. We don't need to teach them the things that writers directly explain; we need to teach them what writers take for granted and do not explain.

There are consequences to understanding that proficient reading is misconceived as a formal skill that doesn't require students to learn taken-for-granted content. When it becomes widely accepted that, on the contrary, reading is *not* a formal skill, and that reading proficiency requires a definable range of specific background knowledge, then we will have to repudiate a whole set of process-oriented, content-indifferent practices in the schools. There is no way around the inherent structural necessity that comprehension entails acquiring the implicitly shared knowledge of the literate speech community. We must teach this shared knowledge to children if they are to become proficient readers.

READING STRATEGIES: A PATH TO BOREDOM

I have observed that American educational theory has been transfixed by the idea of all-purpose how-to strategies, such as "critical thinking" and "inferencing," using as an example Linda Perlstein's account of a school where young students were being subjected to formal reading strategies in an unsuccessful attempt to make them proficient readers when the time would be better spent teaching useful background knowledge. Kate Walsh, in an analysis of existing reading programs, has found that they continually emphasize teaching these conscious formal processes to children from kindergarten through eighth grade, year after year for nine years, classifying, drawing conclusions, making inferences, and predicting outcomes.[29] So much time is being wasted on these misguided activities throughout the nation that if this book manages to persuade even a few teachers and administrators, it will have justified its existence.

One of the favorite exercises is "looking for the main idea." That the idea may be vacuous or useless is apparently less important in these programs than practicing the skill. Here's a typical first-grade story upon which these formal strategies are to be conducted:[30]

What's New in Mrs. Powell's Class?

"It's newsletter time," Mrs. Powell told her class. "What can we tell parents about?"

"The trip to the farm," said Jason.

"And don't forget about the cows running away!" said Danny.

"Good idea," said Mrs. Powell. "What else?"

"The play," said Lola, "so lots of people will come see us."

"Great!" said Mrs. Powell. "Now let's get to work."

Mr. Brown's Farm

We went on a field trip to see Mr. Brown's cows. Mariko forgot to pull the gate shut. All the cows got out. Mr. Brown had to chase them down the road and along the river.

We want to thank Mr. Brown and his cows for a great time. Danny said it really was a field trip because the cows were in the field. Ha ha.

The program then asks the child to summarize the events of this story and "make judgments" about it. But children are not less intelligent than adults, they are just less well informed, and if an adult finds this story empty and pointless, so will a child. If we ask why so much time is being spent on negligible, boring readings, which are offered without coherence from one reading to the next, we are assured by reading experts that the substance of the stories is far less important than the teaching of "metacognitive skills" such as clarifying, "infer-encing," and questioning. These "self-monitoring" skills are supposed to lead more rapidly to reading expertise.

It is true that expert readers do show an ability to find the main idea and to make inferences that aren't in the passage, and, of course, expert readers do these things automatically, without consciously at-tending to the processes. If they *did* consciously attend to such self-monitoring skills, as the young child is being asked to do, they would instantly become less expert in their task, for paying conscious atten-tion to such processes leaves less attentional space for thinking about the implications of the text being read. When expert golfers start pay-ing conscious, "metacognitive" attention to the components of their swing, they clutch. They play badly.[31] There is little scientific reason to expect that expertise in reading can be more quickly and effectively learned through the explicit methods employed in these reading pro-grams, or that the "metacognitive strategies" used by experts are ab-stract, transferable abilities that can be detached from substantive knowledge of the subject matter of the text. We know from large-scale studies that these now universally applied methods do not work. Twenty-five lessons in reading strategies have as little effect as six lessons.[32]

We have already noted that expert readers in one subject are not necessarily expert readers in another. Young children who are nor-mally very inexpert readers will, when confronted with a subject they know something about, manage to show an unaccustomed ability to find the main idea, to make inferences, to classify, and to remember — and all of this to a degree that exceeds the skill of the normally "expert" reader who lacks intimate subject-matter knowledge. A highly knowledgeable reader, young or old, apparently applies many of these skills automatically, not as consciously applied formal strate-gies but in the course of making sense of what is being said in the text.

It is certainly true that at least one of the skills these programs

attempt to teach is consistently central to good comprehension —
"drawing conclusions and making inferences." And it is also true that
experts make inferences much better than novices do. Indeed, of all
the comprehension strategies being taught as formal skills, "inferencing" (the jargon term for inferring) is arguably the most important,
for inference is the essence of comprehension, as cognitive scientists
have amply shown. But the ability to make inferences is not a skill
that is essentially formal in nature. Rather, the kind of inference readers have to make is exemplified in the proposition "All men are mortal; therefore Socrates is mortal." Is that inference justified? Yes, because we supply from our own background knowledge the missing
premise that Socrates is a man. If it happened to be the case that Socrates was a cat, we could not validly make the inference. We are able
to make it not because we have some special "inferencing" skill but
because we know something relevant about Socrates that is unstated
in the text. Inference is filling in a blank in the text that we need to fill
in to understand it. But filling in a blank is not a formal skill; it is not
supplying a missing formal operation. It is supplying a missing substance.

Reading researchers who advocate the extensive teaching of
comprehension strategies are aware of the finding that relevant background knowledge is essential to comprehension, but they take the
position that this doesn't diminish the desirability of strategy instruction, because, they say, young readers do not know how to apply the
background knowledge they already have.[33] This is illustrated, they
say, by the fact that if students are taught consistently to ask "why"
questions about what they read ("questioning the author"), then they
will remember the meaning much better.

That result can just as readily be interpreted as a defense of ordinary subject-matter teaching, since encouraging "why" questions is
the sort of instruction most good teachers use to help students understand and think about something they are reading. I have no dis-
agreement at all with the asking of "why" questions about substantive

readings. It is not, after all, a special strategy instruction; it is normal teaching. I disagree only with the practice of applying this age-old strategy to a series of readings with little cumulative educational value on the principle that learning formal procedures is more important for future reading competency than the actual content being read.

It is true that there is a small *initial* benefit in these strategy exercises for young readers. It's important to explain this initial effect in order to take account of (and not be swayed by) a predictable chorus of claims that research has shown these exercises to be beneficial. For very inexperienced children, explicit practice in "finding the main idea" does help at first, because such exercises help them understand that reading a text is like listening to somebody speak to them. The text is trying to tell them something, just as a person might, and they should try to extract meaning from it in just the way they try to guess what people are driving at when they speak.[34] But this initial benefit in consciously "finding the main idea" quickly levels off. Once children get the idea that a text is like somebody trying to tell them something, they don't have to relearn the principle time after time. Some brief initial strategy instruction is useful because children come to school already possessing oral comprehension skills that are fairly sophisticated. Calling their attention to the way the same skills apply in reading helps them transfer those native skills to reading. But spending more than about six sessions on strategies not only wastes valuable time but actually gets in the way of reading comprehension, since, as cognitive psychologists have suggested, the effort a student devotes to self-consciously finding the main idea is activity that occupies attentional space and subtracts from the child's mental resources available to construct meaning.[35]

Young children do not have to be taught the basics of "inferencing" and other comprehension strategies. Their oral comprehension strategies are already well developed before they come to school. We know that fact because we have one piece of evidence that is decisive. Children have already learned an oral language. The initial process of learning the mother tongue requires each of us to exercise "inferencing skills" that are as demanding as any inferences we will make during the rest of our lives. That is why most first-graders are able to understand even such highly inferential speech conventions as irony and sarcasm ("Man, that's *bad*"), which require subtle comprehension strategies of a high order and are staples of both the suburb and the inner city.[36] It is not mainly comprehension strategies that young children lack in comprehending texts but knowledge — knowledge of formal language conventions and knowledge of the world.

3
KNOWLEDGE OF LANGUAGE

LEARNING THE STANDARD LANGUAGE

To LEARN HOW TO READ and write, children must first know the language of reading and writing — the so-called print code. This language is not always the language spoken in the child's home. Everywhere in the modern world, teaching this print code has become one of the chief functions of schooling. In some places, almost all the children who go to school must learn a language called school speech, which is very different from their home language.[1] Before World War II, in areas of Germany such as Westphalia, people spoke dialects other than those used in print, and young children going to school had to learn the standard German language, Schriftdeutsch. In parts of Africa the difference between school speech and home speech is far greater. Such instances are, in the contemporary world, extreme (and therefore illuminating) examples of the language-learning task that all children must engage in to become proficient readers and writers. We in the United States are not usually aware of the need to learn a special, formal oral language, because the print code that children must learn for reading proficiency here is not a special school language but rather a form of ordinary spoken English called Standard English.

We have possessed this standard language since our nation was born, so we may not realize what an artificial construct it is. The standard national languages of Europe, including English, first became fixed in grammar, spelling, and pronunciation when European nations deliberately codified them in dictionaries in the seventeenth and eighteenth centuries. The standard language of the United States was a variety of the newly standardized language of Great Britain as set forth by, among others, Dr. Johnson in his *Dictionary* of 1755. This was basically the standardized English that was used by Jefferson in the Declaration of Independence and the language in which the Constitution was written. Once a language becomes codified and taught in national school systems, it is very hard to dislodge or change structurally in significant ways. The language of the Declaration is fundamentally the same English that is taught today and that is written and spoken throughout the world.

From the standpoint of learning to read and write, one important difference between this standard print code and several oral dialects of English is that the print code is more conservative, preserving forms that many oral dialects have dropped as unnecessary. For instance, standard written English has preserved like flies in amber certain vestiges, such as the different forms of pronouns and of the verb *to be* — the pronoun pairs *I-me, he-him, she-her* and the verb tenses *am, are, is*. The *I-me* distinction is functionally unnecessary in modern English, which is why so many people get the conventional usage wrong when they say things like "Jim went fishing with John and I." That's incorrect in Standard English, because the prepositional phrase using *with* takes the objective case, *me*, not the nominative, *I*. But in modern English, we don't need different word forms for pronouns, because modern English uses word order to indicate meaning.

Such ancient forms as *I-me* go back to a time when English was an inflected language, like Latin, and indicated grammatical relations by word form, not by word order. But English is no longer like Latin. For example, even though the word forms of *dog* and *man* are the same, we know by word order alone that *The dog bit the man* means something different from *The man bit the dog*. In Old English we could have used either word order to express either meaning, and the words for *dog* and *man* would have had two different forms to express the two different senses. Yet despite the fact that word order now expresses what word form used to express, Standard English has kept the ancient pronouns. We can't say *Me bit the dog*. (Of course, that is just the kind of thing many youngsters do say!) Modern Standard English, based on word order, would be simpler and just as clear if it had only one form of pronouns.

The great linguist Otto Jespersen has pointed out that an increasing simplification is a universal in the history of oral languages and constitutes an improvement in the efficiency of communication.[2] From this point of view, many of the "incorrect" oral dialects of English are superior to the print code. Standard English has *not* consistently evolved toward greater efficiency. That is because all written-down languages, as stored in books and taught in schools, tend to preserve the fixed, written forms. It would have been simpler and more efficient for modern English to apply the word *be* for all present-tense uses, as in *I be, you be, he be, we be, they be*. This familiar oral simplification of the verb *to be* is not a specially distinct feature of so-called Ebonics.[3] The universal *be* has existed for a long time in Great Britain and the United States, because word-order English simply has no need for different word forms. We don't need *am, is, are*. With English verbs, as with its pronouns, a single form can very well do the work of all, without ambiguity. No matter. We are now stuck with *am, are, is*, and this old-fashioned print English is now being learned and taught all over the world. It exists in millions of books and magazines and is broadcast to billions of people. It is pretty safe to predict that *am, is, are, him, her*, etc. will be with us as long as English is. Children need to learn these and all of the standard forms of the print code accurately in order to learn reading, writing, and formal speaking.

With the passage of time and the spread of schooling, this American school speech, the print code, gradually became the ordinary language of many homes in the United States — especially in homes where school-educated adults came to use the standard, school-based language in their everyday speech. Some children arrive at school with fairly large vocabularies and a well-practiced sense of the standard forms and the complex sentence constructions that characterize formal speech and the language of writing. These children already have a sense of the formal print code.[4] Other, less well prepared children come to school needing to learn this formal style of speech. In view of recent (not always linguistically informed) controversies over dialects and the inhibiting effect these controversies have had on schools and teachers, schools should emphasize the manufactured character of the standard language and at the same time its absolute necessity in reading and writing. The standard language has to be learned as part of learning to read and write.

LEARNING GRAMMAR

Parents and teachers should ignore the "expert" advice that holds that it is unnecessary to teach children grammar. This is a grave mistake, because grammar in the early grades is essentially learning the names of the parts of speech: nouns, pronouns, verbs, adjectives, adverbs, prepositions, conjunctions, and interjections. These and a few other terms serve as a means of talking about language with children. It is not necessary to teach grammar as an abstract subject to third-graders. But in order to discuss language efficiently, teachers and parents need to name the parts of speech and a few other terms, like *subject, predicate, direct object, indirect object, prepositional phrase, singular, plural,* and *agreement.* Such names are critical teaching devices, because, as we've seen, Standard English uses highly unnecessary differences in word forms like *I* and *me* or *she* and *her.* In order to teach children the conventions of the print code efficiently, we need to tell them explicitly that *I* is a subject and *me* is an object. We don't want them to be scorned for incorrect usage by language snobs, but there is more at stake: it is an equity issue that affects children's economic future and capacity to gain respect. To tell children how to get these unnecessary forms right, we must use the grammatical names, and children must know what they mean.

In recent decades, emotionally charged controversies over standard versus nonstandard speech have inhibited schools from emphasizing the formal, standard modes of pronunciation, syntax, and grammar.[5] Because the subject elicits emotions and conflicts, many schools and textbooks have deemphasized teaching these standard forms of grammar and pronunciation intensively. This has been convenient for adults but is a misfortune for many children. It has hindered proficiency in the formal print code among disadvantaged children — and among advantaged children as well, for they too must learn to master the formal modes of speech that are used in print. In the United States, the standard language that one needs to become a proficient reader and writer is not restricted to print, as we've seen. It is also the formal language people use in everyday discourse when conversing with strangers. It is the language of the job interview, the public oration, the TV or radio broadcast, and the classroom.

The controversies over teaching the standard language too often neglect these linguistic facts.[6] A number of claims against standard grammatical syntax and pronunciation have been launched in recent decades. Textbook writers and teachers have been told that research has proved that all dialects are equal, that grammar study is unnecessary, and that the imposition of the standard language is a form of cultural imperialism.[7] Some experts have suggested that school ought to be conducted in the language of the home, as in the well-known controversy over Ebonics.[8] Because that view was contrary to common sense, the controversy was short-lived, but the issue it raised was not, and it has continued to be debated in overt or submerged form since the 1960s. The National Council of Teachers of English recently (in 2003) reaffirmed the position taken in its 1974 manifesto, titled "Students' Right to Their Own Language."

Many of the impulses behind these claims — respecting diverse forms of speech and home backgrounds — are honorable, and many of the recent controversies concern the relative esteem in which various forms of speech should be held in the larger society. Telling children that their home speech is somehow inferior sends the cruel message that these children and their homes are inferior too, a disparagement that, besides inflicting psychological damage, could very well discourage them from enthusiastically learning the language of reading and writing. No good school or teacher wants to send such a harmful message. The controversies have been useful to the extent that they cause teachers to be respectfully sensitive to language diversity and to make very clear that different language forms are used in different places. One has to learn when and where to use different language forms, just as one needs to learn what kind of clothes to wear on different occasions. It's part of one's education.

LEARNING THE ELABORATED CODE

Equally essential to children's reading and writing is mastery of the structural differences between formal and informal speech. This is not a difference between spoken and written language. It is basically a difference between two kinds of spoken language — the difference between speech addressed to intimates and speech addressed to strangers. Reading and writing require mastery of the kinds of speech used to speak to strangers rather than to intimates. Young children go to school knowing how to talk and listen at home; they need to learn how to talk and listen in the wider world.

The British sociolinguist Basil Bernstein brought intellectual clarity to this subject by labeling one kind of home talk (found most often among less well educated people) with the term "restricted code" and more printlike talk (found most often among educated people) with the term "elaborated code."[9] The difference between restricted and elaborated codes is structural. The restricted code is brief; it is addressed to intimates; it takes for granted a lot of unspoken situational and shared background knowledge. It's a code that says simply "Move," rather than "Jimmy, will you please get out of Daddy's chair? He needs to rest." (Bernstein's observations are supported by other researchers, who noted that the home utterances heard by children with educated parents are fuller and more complex than the utterances heard by children with less well educated parents.)[10] The restricted code is more implicit than explicit; it leaves a great deal unsaid. The sociolinguist William Labov criticized Bernstein for suggesting by the word *restricted* that this mode of speech conveys less than formal speech does, pointing out that oral speech is just more concentrated.[11] That is a fair objection, but Bernstein's other term, "elaborated code," is incontrovertibly useful. It very accurately describes the kind of school speech that children need to learn.

One of the experiments Bernstein described used a set of cartoons that depicted some soccer-playing children who accidentally sent a ball through someone's living room window, to the annoyance of the homeowner. The researchers showed the pictures to young children with uneducated and with educated parents and asked them to describe what was happening in the drawings. Bernstein, a sociologist, called the children's homes "lower-class" and "middle-class." A typical answer from the lower-class homes was "They're playing football [soccer], and he kicks it, and it goes through there." By contrast, the typical response of children from middle-class homes who grew up speaking the print code started out "Three boys are playing football, and one boy kicks the ball, and it goes through the window."[12]

In the first response, the restricted code could communicate everything that was communicated in the elaborated code — as long as the listener had the same context knowledge that the speaker had, which was the case when both were looking at the same drawing. By contrast, the middle-class children's response in the elaborated code did not assume as much shared background knowledge. Even in the absence of the drawing, their response could communicate to strangers, since it provided more explicit context knowledge stated in more explicit language. Because the elaborated code is less dependent than ordinary speech on a rich, immediately shared situational context, it is the mode of speech that is essential for formal oral discourse and for reading and writing.

Lessons in receiving and producing the conventions of the standard language and the elaborated code are just as important to later reading and writing as a careful sequence of lessons in the mechanics of decoding and encoding an alphabetic script. These lessons in talking and listening can take various forms, but they should consistently include regular oral performance so each child can learn and practice the conventions of using the formal, elaborated code of public speech and expository writing. Practice in speaking before an audience, even if the child is pretending at home or even if he speaks briefly as part of the discussion period in class, will help produce strong later gains in reading and writing proficiency, and also in the ability to communicate with strangers on an equal footing.

BUILDING VOCABULARY

If learning the print code is critical to children's reading and writing ability, so is having an adequate vocabulary. The process of learning words, one of the most studied and interesting topics in psychology, is still incompletely understood. We know that children gain vocabulary in fits and starts, with advances and retreats and slow progress in small increments along a broad front. It's reminiscent of the process that Darwin traced in the most popular book of his lifetime, about the slow but sure contribution of the earthworm to the English garden.[13] On a given day the earthworm doesn't do much to help the soil of the garden (or the woodland or field). But day after day of ingesting soil, excreting it, adding to its structure, its organic matter, and its homogeneity; day after day, year after year of bringing bits from below — in time, these imperceptible changes add up to big results that transform unthrifty soil into a nourishing, water-retentive milieu for the roots of plants. We gain word meanings by a similarly slow, accretive process. Vocabulary gains in a day may not be easily detectable. The gains of a year may not accurately register on standardized tests. But we can speed progress. To the earthworm can be added the plow. Since schooling takes up only a portion of children's language experience, every effort should be made to make vocabulary-building in school as effective as possible.

Comprehending a text depends on knowing the meanings of most of its words. Vocabulary growth, which is a slow process that gradually accumulates a very large number of words, must be fostered intensively in the earliest grades if we are to bring all children to proficiency in reading as quickly as possible. That a person can learn up to fifteen new words a day from age two to age seventeen is one of the most remarkable feats of the human mind. Even though how we do it remains something of a psychological mystery, through recent work we have learned enough about vocabulary growth to formulate some conclusions about the most productive means of enlarging children's vocabularies, especially among students whose initial vocabularies are relatively small.

The psycholinguist Steven Pinker has argued on the basis of persuasive evidence that two separate language functions exist in the human mind, one for words and one for rules.[14] The rules include grammatical and other conventions that concern the forms of utterances. Once learned, they can be applied to most speech. For example, the rule for the grammatical form of most plurals in English is to add an s. Word meanings are not like that; they are not rule-governed; they need to be learned individually. No rule instructs us to use the word *pencil* to denote a particular kind of object. We just have to learn the word and remember it.

Word learning takes place most efficiently when the reader or listener already understands the context well. Researchers have found that we learn the words of a foreign language most effectively when the subject matter is familiar.[15] If you read in French that "Lyon a battu Lille," you will make greater gains in learning what *battu* means if you know something about soccer. This finding appeals to common sense. You can guess accurately what the word ought to mean in the context, because you know what is being talked about. This picture is supported by recent research, which shows that we infer the meanings of words by grasping the whole meaning of the utterance in the form of a mental situation model. If we are hearing a story about a fire team putting out a fire and we first encounter the word *flames,* we can make a good guess about what it means, because we understand the situation referred to in the sentence in which *flames* is used. We must grasp this whole situation (precisely or vaguely) when we understand what is said or written. This understanding of the whole context is the basis for guessing the meanings of new words.

This fact explains why we learn words up to four times faster in a familiar than in an unfamiliar context.[16] This finding is inherently plausible, since we learn new words by guessing what they mean in the context, and these guesses are likely to be faster and more accurate if we are familiar with the kinds of situation being referred to. An optimal early reading program will exploit this characteristic of word learning by ensuring that the topics of reading and discussion are consistent over several class periods, so the topic becomes familiar to the students and thus accelerates word learning.

The Matthew effect in reading, whereby the rich get richer and the poor poorer, is inevitable in the case of vocabulary. Those who know more words will learn still more by virtue of that fact, while those who know few words will gain new ones at a slower rate. As we've seen, experts say that we need to know about 90 to 95 percent of a text's words to understand it.[17] Children who already have sufficient word knowledge will understand the text and will therefore guess the meanings of the other 10 percent of the words. They shall have abundance. But those who know only 70 percent of the words will neither understand the text nor gain insight into the other 30 percent. They will see not, neither will they understand. Now, after looking at the text, they are further behind the advantaged group than they were before they read the text. If this pattern continues, the gap between the two groups will grow with each successive language experience. This is exactly what currently happens in our schools. Failing to construct meaning, these children fail to learn new words. Such unrewarding experiences also tend to induce a dislike and avoidance of reading, so the child falls even further behind.

An adequate early vocabulary is therefore fateful for later reading achievement. Other things being equal, the earlier children acquire a large vocabulary, the greater their reading comprehension will be in later grades. Anne Cunningham and Keith Stanovich have shown that under current conditions of American schooling, vocabulary in second grade is a reliable predictor of academic performance in eleventh grade.[18] They have also shown that the biggest contribution to the size of any person's vocabulary must come from the printed page (whether it is heard or read), because print uses a greater number of different words than everyday oral speech does.[19] Since children in early grades can't read these materials effectively for themselves, they should be read to. Reading aloud to very young children is one of the main agents of their vocabulary progress.

Vocabulary enhancement is not quite as emotionally charged and controversial as teaching the standard language — except to vocabulary experts. There has raged for at least three decades a polite war between those who favor increasing students' vocabulary mainly through intense exposure to rich language (interspersed with brief discussion of word meanings when essential) and those who favor spending a fairly significant portion of class time on the explicit study of word meanings.[20] The implicit-learning proponents say that children will gain a large vocabulary faster by spending time listening to and reading interesting materials. The explicit-learning proponents say that systematic word study yields faster results. This is an important debate on which schools need to take a position if they are to institute an effective language arts program.

At issue is time allocation. Both parties agree that an ideal program includes some measure of both implicit and explicit vocabulary learning. But if twenty to thirty minutes a day are devoted to focused, explicit word study, that cumulative time, which might have been spent in other ways, can make a big difference over the course of a year or two — especially if it turns out that students can make more progress in vocabulary by devoting that time to a less explicit approach. The fact that the debate over this issue continues suggests that we may not yet have enough direct data to decide the question. But we do have a good deal of indirect data — enough to offer some definite advice to parents and teachers on this subject.[21]

Let's consider some raw numbers. All parties to the implicit-explicit debate agree that even when teachers spend up to thirty minutes a day in explicit word study, the maximum number of new words they can teach this way during a school year is about four hundred.[22] Compare that number to the average of two thousand to five thousand words per year that an advantaged child will have learned from age two to age seventeen. It is clear from these ballpark figures that most of our word learning occurs indirectly, through hearing, reading, and understanding a lot of text and talk. The consensus of *all* researchers is that indirect, implicit learning is by far the main mode of increasing one's vocabulary.

To say that children learn a definite number of words during a day or a year is of course to present a completely oversimplified model of what actually goes on in word learning. First of all, there is no such thing as knowing the meaning of a word, for most words in actual use do not have an unchanging, definite meaning. They are multipurpose tools that adapt to different occasions. They take on different meanings in different uses. This multiplicity of meanings is indicated by dictionary definitions that list multiple senses of many words. But those dictionary lists are far from complete. The listed definitions are at best hints of what a word may mean in an actual use. The general sense of a word that a listener or reader gains from experiencing actual uses of the word is not a fixed and definite meaning but general meaning, possibilities and probabilities that get narrowed down through context. Each new exposure to the word in a new context can subtly alter that constantly accruing system of probabilities and possibilities.[23] Researchers have found that we need multiple exposures to a word in multiple contexts to start getting a secure sense of its overtones and range. That is why word learning is inherently a slow and gradual process. We do not learn so many discrete words a day. Rather, we are learning small, incremental aspects of hundreds of words in a day, along a broad front, as we understand whole utterances in context. It appears that we have a remarkable innate faculty for learning word meanings in context.[24] This fact, more than any other, is shifting scientific opinion in the direction of those who favor implicit word learning as the more efficient method of increasing a person's vocabulary.

One reason for the long-standing learned debate over this issue has been that the conclusion favoring an implicit approach seems inconsistent with much else that we know about human learning. An explicit approach is usually more efficient. That initially suggests that proponents of explicit instruction could well be right. For example, explicit instruction plus guided practice is the most efficient way of teaching students how to map the forty-odd phonemes of English onto the twenty-six letters of the alphabet in some hundred-plus ways. The superiority of an explicit, analytical method in this case has been amply shown.[25] And there are many other examples of the superior efficiency of explicit, focused instruction. How astonishing, then, if it should turn out that the most efficient way of learning thousands of word meanings is through an unconscious, automatic, and implicit process. Yet the weight of evidence indicates it is so. The proponents of naturalism in learning are not always wrong, it appears. It depends on what is to be learned.[26]

In this instance there is a big psychological difference between learning word meanings and learning how to decode the sounds of letters. The child who goes to school having learned hundreds of words simply by being exposed to language finds it difficult to map the forty-odd sounds of Standard English onto twenty-six letters simply by being exposed to print and pictures. The implicit method of learning the alphabet code fails with many students, just as it failed mankind throughout history, until Phoenician scholars worked out the alphabetic principle. But for children who find it impossible to learn the alphabetic code by implicit means, the task of implicitly learning thousands of word meanings just by being exposed to a lot of articulated noises is like falling off a log. It appears that a different learning mechanism is at work for gradually acquiring the meanings of words. A plausible explanation is that we humans don't possess a built-in alphabet-phoneme-mapping faculty but we do possess a built-in word-meaning-learning faculty.

Thomas Landauer and his colleagues have modeled this complex faculty in computer programs that can be taught word use from context in a manner and at a rate similar to humans — without even having the benefit of knowing what the words mean. Landauer's is a complex computational program that gauges probabilities of use from both the presence and the absence of words in various types of context. In his view, our remarkable language ability seems to be an adaptation of a more general automatic probability-computing ability in the brain. It seems that this computational feature has become particularly well adapted to learning word-meaning probabilities and possibilities.[27] Landauer may be right. Certainly the results of his computer modeling are impressive.

Another, and perhaps more plausible, model of this word-learning capacity, which does not depend on rapid computational abilities that we (unlike computers) may not in fact possess, has been offered by George A. Miller. He suggests that we remember instances and pieces of context when we experience words, so that our memory of the word carries bits of varied contexts with it. These become activated selectively, depending on the current context. When we understand the sense of a word, part of what we understand is the larger context in which the word typically occurs when it has that sense. The word *shot* has a different sense on the golf course and in a bar, and these different senses carry with them pieces of these contexts.[28] This inherently contextualized meaning cannot be effectively taught outside the meaning-lending context, which is another reason that sticking to a context and focusing on subject matter is the surest and fastest way to learn new words.

Before Landauer and his colleagues published their highly mathematical work, Richard Anderson, Patricia Herman, and William Nagy had suggested a more generalized, easy-to-understand quantitative principle that explains why implicit word learning appears to be more efficient than explicit word learning. Their famous article used the following argument: When we consciously study a specific word — say the word *nimble*, as in "Jack be nimble, Jack be quick" — we are focusing attention on that word. It may be true that we will make faster progress in learning that one word by seeing focused and repeated examples than by just being exposed to it once or twice in the course of listening or reading. But if we did not focus on that word, Nagy, Herman, and Anderson point out, we would be trying to get some sense of a dozen or more words. And so they raise the question, is it best to make tiny gains on a dozen words or big gains on just one? In the long run, which method leads to most word learning? On the whole, the implicit method, they suggest, is best.[29]

Although the weight of evidence points clearly away from focused vocabulary work, explicit vocabulary study carries a benefit when it is done judiciously as an aid to creating an understood context. If we are reading to children a story about a wolf and a rabbit and the author says that the wolf is a carnivore, should we just let the children figure out what the word means from the context? No! This word is crucial to understanding the story. Then and there, we should explain the word briefly so the children will understand the rest of the story. In this case, a judicious use of explicit explanation enhances the main work of implicit word learning by making the context more familiar for the other words the children encounter. It's clear that a sparing use of well-contextualized explicit meaning instruction is useful for vocabulary gain. More extended explicit word study is probably inefficient in the long run.

Can Disadvantaged Children Catch Up?

Let's return to the subject of speeding up word learning for disadvantaged children. For an advantaged child, the figure of ten to fifteen new words a day is, as I've explained, highly misleading as a description of the actual process of word learning. It is an average number, arrived at by taking the number of words that a superior student knows at age seventeen and dividing that number by the number of days the student has lived from age two to age seventeen. But the curve of word learning is not a straight line. We don't learn the same number of words every year. The number of new words gained per unit of time is rather small at age two, and it rises with each succeeding year. In later life, when people already know most of the words they hear and read, the number of new words they gain per year slows down again.

This nonlinear pattern of vocabulary growth allows us to make a hopeful qualification of the Matthew effect in reading comprehension. Vocabulary growth is not entirely like the growth of money in an interest-bearing bank account. Suppose the interest on money is compounded at 5 percent a year. Somebody who starts out with just $10 in an account will fall further and further behind somebody who starts out with $100. After ten years, the initial difference of $90 will become a larger difference of $146. That is because the rates stay the same for both accounts and the supply of money is not limited. That pattern, unfortunately, describes what is currently happening in our schools. The vocabulary gap between advantaged and disadvantaged students widens the longer they stay in our schools. Potentially, though, vocabulary growth can work in a less Matthew-like way, because the rates of vocabulary growth in the two students do not have to be identical. If a student who is behind in word knowledge can be brought to know 90 percent of the words that she hears and reads in school, then she can pick up new words at a faster rate than the advantaged student who already knows 98 percent of the words.

Besides this structural possibility for narrowing the vocabulary gap, there is a further opportunity for catching up, which depends on the special richness of the vocabulary that is studied in school. That is because the vocabulary heard in school is potentially richer than the vocabulary heard outside school. Oral speech tends to use a smaller vocabulary than written speech.[30] Almost all of the rare words that we know have been gained from print — print read either silently or aloud.[31] If school conditions provide enough context familiarity to speed up the learning of these rarer words for all groups, then the relative gain by the disadvantaged groups will be greater and the gap will be narrowed. Large-scale data in French research support this prediction. After several years of schooling (studies in France indicate that the effect becomes manifest around grade five), a good system of schooling can begin to overcome a disadvantaged student's initial vocabulary deficit.[32]

4
KNOWLEDGE OF THINGS

WHAT THE TEXT DOESN'T SAY

CONSIDER THE FOLLOWING sentence, which is one that most literate Americans can understand but most literate English people cannot, even when they have a wide vocabulary and know the conventions of the standard language:

> Jones sacrificed and knocked in a run.

Typically, a literate English person would know all the words yet wouldn't comprehend the sentence. (In fairness, most Americans would be equally baffled by a sentence about the sport of cricket.) To understand this sentence about Jones and his sacrifice, you need a wealth of relevant background knowledge that goes beyond vocabulary and syntax — relevant knowledge that is far broader than the words of the sentence present. Let's consider what we as writers would have to convey to an English person to make this sentence comprehensible. (To avoid making this an entire chapter about baseball, the explanation won't go the whole way.)

First, we would have to explain that Jones was at bat. That would entail an explanation of the inning system and the three-outs system. It would entail an explanation of the size and shape of the baseball field (necessary to the concept of a sacrifice fly or bunt), which would require a digression on what a fly or a bunt is. The reader would also have to have some vague sense of the layout of the bases, how many there are, and what a run is. The English person would need to be given a sense of how the pitching team is positioned on the field and how many of them there are. That would require a gloss on the pitcher and the difference between balls and strikes, which would require at least a vague idea of where the strike zone is. At that point we would have gotten started, but by the time an English reader had begun to assimilate all this relevant background knowledge, he or she may have lost track of the whole point of the explanation. What was the original sentence? It will have been submerged in a flurry of additional sentences branching out in different directions.

That it should take so much time to explain a simple sentence containing not a single unfamiliar vocabulary word illustrates the impracticality of the idea that people can simply strategize what a sentence means or look up the knowledge they need for reading comprehension. Time considerations alone require that the background knowledge needed to fill in the blanks must be quickly and readily available to the reader's mind.

The example also illustrates a feature of reading and writing that we touched on in discussing Basil Bernstein's distinction between an elaborated and a restricted code. In ordinary oral speech — for example, in a conversation at an actual baseball game — the whole meaning of our sentence might be conveyed in the restricted code by two words: "He sacrificed." We wouldn't need to say "Jones," because we already know who is batting. We wouldn't need to say that he knocked in a run, since we would know that too. The only aspect worthy of explicit comment might be that Jones intended to do what he did. The original sentence, "Jones sacrificed and knocked in a run," is far more explicit than "He sacrificed." Nonetheless, it still isn't elaborated enough for a typical English person.

Just how elaborated does writing have to be in order for the general reader to understand it? The answer to that question yields an answer to a key question about improving students' reading comprehension: what knowledge do students need to gain to become good readers?

WHO IS THE GENERAL READER?

Recently I was reading out loud a wonderful Robert McCloskey book to a four-year-old. The book, called *Burt Dow: Deep-Water Man,* is about a retired sea captain who goes fishing and encounters a whale. The reading was not a success. The pictures are marvelous, but the text is intended for a more experienced and knowledgeable reader than that four-year-old was — at the least it needed a four-year-old who lives near the sea and boats and knows what *rigging* and *gunnels* and *sou'wester* are, not to mention *planking* and *weather eye.* A request was made to engage in another activity. It wasn't McCloskey's fault. Many older children and grownups, even if they are not experienced sailors, can understand and delight in his book. Its sense is available to a reader who is neither an expert nor a complete novice in matters of the sea, just as the Jones sentence is directed at someone who is not a complete novice about baseball. Both texts are directed to a "general reader."

The idea of the general reader is a structurally necessary one that enables mass communication to occur.[1] The printed text always takes something for granted, always leaves blanks to be filled in by the reader to make it comprehensible.[2] Unless writers and their readers internalize the shared knowledge of the wider speech community (such as shared knowledge about baseball), they cannot expect the blanks to be filled in; they cannot be successful writers or proficient readers.

Yet these ideas are rarely, if ever, mentioned in reading programs. That is yet another illustration of the degree to which current thinking about reading is trapped in formalistic conceptions that regard texts as found objects rather than as historically dependent writings which assume the existence of widely shared background knowledge within a particular speech community.

A creature from Mars who had learned the rules of Standard English and the words of a dictionary plus comprehension strategies still could not read the *New York Times*, or a computer instruction manual, or *Gone With the Wind*. The Martian would be in the same predicament as the English person reading about baseball. He would not have enough relevant background knowledge to form an accurate situation model. This point was empirically demonstrated some years ago during the cold war, when hundreds of millions of dollars were spent in developing computer programs that could automatically translate Russian into English. The dollars were wasted, because the project was based on an inadequate theory, which assumed that computers needed only formal language rules, dictionary word meanings, and comprehension strategies to translate meaning. The computer translation scheme began to be more workable when researchers started supplying the computers with a large knowledge base relevant to the subjects being translated.[3]

Every newspaper and book editor and every producer for radio and TV is conscious of the need to distinguish what can be taken for granted from what must be explained. Learning the craft of writing is bound up with learning how to gauge what can be assumed versus what must be explained. The general reader that every journalist or TV newscaster must imagine is somebody whose relevant knowledge is assumed to lie between the total ignorance of a complete novice and the detailed knowledge of an expert. A newspaper baseball story cannot assume an audience as uninformed about the game as our imagined English person or one consisting of baseball experts. Every person who speaks and writes must make an estimate of what can be left unexplained and what must be explicitly stated. Being able to make such an estimate is part of our general communicative competence, and it is therefore something all our children need to be taught. Reading proficiency, listening proficiency, speaking proficiency, and writing proficiency all require possession of the broad knowledge that the general reader is assumed to have and also the understanding that others can be expected to possess that knowledge.

We said that this topic of taken-for-granted knowledge, which is absolutely essential to reading and writing, is neglected in current reading programs. Yet not to teach the knowledge that is taken for granted in formal discourse systematically is equivalent to neglecting to teach a tennis beginner that the ball has to go over the net and stay inside the lines. Most current reading programs talk about activating the reader's background knowledge so she can comprehend a text. But in practice, they are only paying lip service to the well-known scientific finding that background knowledge is essential to reading comprehension. Little attempt is made to enlarge the child's background knowledge. The disjointed topics and stories that one finds in current reading programs seem designed mainly to appeal to the knowledge that young readers may already have, such as "Going to School" and "Jenny at the Supermarket." The programs do not make a systematic effort to convey coherently, grade by grade, the knowledge that newspapers, magazines, and serious radio and TV programs assume American readers and listeners possess.

Referring to the knowledge that American readers are assumed to possess is another way of saying that the range of specific knowledge needed to be a proficient reader is different among American readers than it is among readers in other nations — a point I tried to illustrate in the baseball example. That is why we speak of the tacit knowledge within a particular speech community — of the knowledge assumed to be known by Americans. In the modern world, the background knowledge a person needs for good reading comprehension tends to be largely (but by no means entirely) national in character. For publications in English, American and English (and Canadian, Australian, and New Zealand) newspaper readers take for granted slightly different ranges of knowledge. The range of assumed knowledge is different among Chinese and Russian newspaper readers and speakers, and so on.

How Much Knowledge Do We Need?

Here is the first paragraph of an article by Janet Maslin, taken at random from the books section of the *New York Times* on February 6, 2003. It is an example of writing addressed to a general reader that a literate American high school graduate would be expected to understand.

> When Luca Turin was a boy growing up in Paris, according to Chandler Burr's ebullient new book about him, "he was famous for boring everyone to death with useless, disconnected facts, like the distance between the earth and the moon in Egyptian cubits." Mr. Burr sets out to explain how such obsessive curiosity turned Mr. Turin into a pioneering scientist who, in the author's estimation, deserves a Nobel Prize.

This example shows that the background knowledge required to understand the general sections of the *New York Times*, such as the book review section, is not deep. It is not that of an expert — of course not, for we cannot all be experts on the diverse subjects that are treated by books. If authors want their books to be sold and read, they must not assume that their readers are experts. They may take for granted only the relevant background knowledge that a literate audience can be expected to possess.

What *do* readers need to know in order to comprehend this passage? We need to know first that this is a book review, which aims to tell us what the book is about and whether it is worth reading. We need to understand that the reviewer is favorably disposed to the book, calling it "ebullient," and that it is a nonfiction work about a scientist named Luca Turin. We need to have at least a vague semantic grasp of key words like *ebullient, boring, obsessive, pioneering, estimation*. We need to know some of the things mentioned with exactness, but not others. It's not necessary to know how long a cubit is. Indeed, the text implies that this is an odd bit of information, and we can infer that it is some form of measurement. (Maslin may assume that we remember that the word is used in the Bible story of Noah's Ark.) We need to know in general what Paris is, what the moon is and that it circles the earth, that it is not too far away in celestial terms, and we need to have some idea what a Nobel Prize is and that it is very prestigious. Consider the knowledge domains included in this list. Paris belongs to history and geography; so does Egypt. The moon belongs to astronomy and natural history. The Nobel Prize belongs to general history and science.

We may infer from this example that only a person with broad general knowledge is capable of reading with understanding the *New York Times* and other newspapers. This fact has momentous implications for education, and for democracy as well. A universal ability of citizens to read newspapers or their equivalent with understanding is the essence of democracy. Jefferson put the issue unforgettably: "The basis of our government being the opinion of the people, the very first object should be to keep that right; and were it left to me to decide whether we should have a government without newspapers or newspapers without a government, I should not hesitate a moment to prefer the latter. But I should mean that every man should receive those papers and be capable of reading them."[4] The last phrase, "be capable of reading them," is often omitted from the quotation, but it is the crucial one. Reading achievement will not advance significantly until schools recognize and act on the fact that it depends on the possession of a broad but definable range of diverse knowledge. The effective teaching of reading will require schools to teach the diverse, enabling knowledge that reading requires.

WHICH KNOWLEDGE DO WE NEED?

But what exactly does that enabling knowledge consist of? That is the nuts-and-bolts question. The practical problem of helping all students achieve adequate reading comprehension skills will depend on our schools being able to narrow down what seems at first glance to be vast amounts of heterogeneous information into a teachable repertory that will enable students to understand the diverse texts that are addressed to a general reader. Our sketch of the background knowledge needed to understand Maslin's short passage offers clues to the kind of instruction that is needed to advance general reading comprehension ability. It will be broad instruction in the worlds of nature and culture as a necessary platform for gaining deeper knowledge through listening and reading. But what should that broad general knowledge be?

It is assumed by the American educational community that any "representative" knowledge will do.[5] My colleagues Joseph Kett and James Trefil and I set out to develop more useful guidance for schools than this imprecise and inaccurate notion back in the 1980s. We asked ourselves, "In the American context, what knowledge is taken for granted in the classroom, in public orations, in serious radio and TV, in books and magazines and newspapers addressed to a general audience?" We considered various scholarly approaches to this problem. One was to look at word frequencies. If a word appeared in print quite often, then it was probably a word whose meaning was not going to be explained by the speaker or writer. We looked at a frequency analysis of the Brown Corpus, a collection of passages from very diverse kinds of publications that was lodged at Brown University, but we found that this purely mechanical approach, while partially valid, did not yield altogether accurate or intelligent results. For example, because the Brown Corpus was compiled in the 1950s, "Nikita Khrushchev" was a more frequent vocabulary item than "George Washington."[6]

Another shortcoming of this "objective" approach was its failure to discriminate between language and knowledge, that is, between words and what they refer to. That shortcoming is apparent in the sentence about Jones and his sacrifice. Knowing the basic meaning of the word *sacrifice* does not suffice if one is reading the sentence. A mechanical, purely language-based approach to the needed knowledge is inherently misleading. A much better way of finding out what knowledge speakers and writers take for granted is to ask these people themselves whether they assume specific items of knowledge in what they read and write. This direct approach proved to be a sounder way of determining the tacit knowledge, because what we must teach students is the knowledge that proficient readers and writers actually use. From people in every region of the country we found a reassuring amount of agreement on the substance of this taken-for-granted knowledge.

We had predicted this agreement. The very nature of communicative competence, a skill that teachers, reporters, doctors, lawyers, book club members, and writers have already shown themselves to have, requires that it be widely shared within the speech community. These are successful communicators, and shared, taken-for-granted background knowledge is what makes successful communication possible. Several years after our compilation of such knowledge was published, independent researchers investigated whether reading comprehension ability did in fact depend on knowledge of the topics we had set forth. The studies showed an unambiguous correlation between knowledge of these topics and reading comprehension scores, school grades, and other indexes of reading skill. One researcher investigated whether the topics we set forth as taken-for-granted items are in fact taken for granted in newspaper texts addressed to a general reader. He examined the *Times* by computer over a period of 101 months and found that "any given day's issue of the *Times* contained approximately 2,700 occurrences" of these unexplained terms, which "play a part in the daily commerce of the published language."[7]

An inventory of the tacit knowledge shared by good readers and writers cannot, of course, be fixed at a single point in time. The knowledge that writers and radio and TV personalities take for granted is constantly changing at the edges, especially on topical issues. But inside the edges, at the core, the body of assumed knowledge in American public discourse has remained stable for many decades.[8] Only students who are conversant with this assumed knowledge can understand more specialized matter. This core of knowledge changes very slowly, as sociolinguists have pointed out. If we want to bring all students to reading proficiency, this stable core is the enabling knowledge that we must teach.

That's more easily said than done. One essential, preliminary question that we faced was, how can this necessary knowledge be sequenced in a practical way for use in schools? We asked teachers how to present these topics grade by grade and created working groups of experienced teachers in every region of the country to produce a sequence independently of the others. There proved to be less agreement on how to present the material grade by grade than there had been in identifying what the critical topics are. That difficulty too was predicted, since the sequencing of many topics is inherently arbitrary. While it's plausible in math that addition needs to come before multiplication and that in history Greece probably ought to come before Rome, maybe it's not plausible that Greece should come before George Washington.

We collected the accumulated wisdom of these independent groups of teachers, made a provisional draft sequence, and in 1990 held a conference where 145 people from every region, scholarly discipline, and racial and ethnic group got together to work extremely hard for two and a half days to agree on an intelligent way to teach this knowledge sequentially. Over time, this Core Knowledge Sequence has been refined and adjusted, based on actual classroom experience. It is now used in several hundred schools (with positive effects on reading scores), and it is distinguished among content standards not only for its interest and richness, but also because of the carefully-thought-out scientific foundations that underlie the selection of topics.[9]

Why Not in the Reading Program?

But while the general course of study outlined in the Core Knowledge Sequence (which focuses on history, science, and the arts as disciplines but lacks a reading program per se) is bound to improve reading comprehension in the long term, a great opportunity is being lost when this efficient and coherent approach to the knowledge required for reading is being neglected in the very place where it is most needed — namely, in the long hours devoted to the subject of reading. Since at least ninety minutes per day are currently allotted to reading in early grades, about an hour could be devoted to the language and world knowledge that is most important for competence in listening, talking, reading, and writing. The substantive topics in literature, history, the arts, and the sciences that literate Americans take for granted are deeply interesting and highly engaging to children.

For many years, the great reading researcher Jeanne Chall complained that the selections offered in language arts classes did not provide students with the knowledge and language experiences they need for general competence in reading. She observed that far too much time was being spent on trivial, ephemeral fictions and far too little on diverse nonfictional genres. In the two decades since Chall entered this complaint, little has changed. Most current programs still assume that language arts is predominantly about "literature," which is conceived as poems and fictional stories, often trivial ones meant to be inoffensive vehicles for teaching formal skills. Stories are indeed the best vehicles for teaching young children — an idea that was ancient when Plato reasserted it in *Republic*. But stories are not necessarily the same things as ephemeral fictions. Many an excellent story is told about real people and events, and even stories that are fictional take much of their worth from the nonfictional truths about the world that they convey.

The association of language arts mainly with fiction and poetry is an accident of recent intellectual history that is not inherent in the nature of things. Older American texts that were designed to teach reading, such as the McGuffey Readers, contained moral tales and historical narratives as well as fictional stories (not that we should go back to the McGuffey Readers, which have many shortcomings). Ideally, a good language arts program in the early grades will contain not only fiction and poetry but also narratives about the real worlds of nature and history. Ideally, such a program will fit in with and reinforce a well-planned overall curriculum in history, science, and the arts. The recent finding that word learning occurs much faster in a familiar context implies that the overall program should stay on a subject-matter domain long enough to make it familiar. As we've seen, such integration of content in reading and subject-matter classes will serve simultaneously to enrich background knowledge and enlarge vocabulary in an optimal way.

That fictional stories can convey factual and moral truths is the traditional ground for defending their value and importance in education. The truth-telling and knowledge-enhancing aspect of fiction is emphatically just as important as the aspect of fiction and poetry that stimulates children's imaginations. The romantic idea that literature should mainly nurture the imagination fits in well with the generally romantic flavor of early childhood education in the United States today. I do not wish to appear in any way hostile to developing children's imaginations. But the second- and third-rate fictions that are too often presented to children in the early grades are far less stimulating to their imaginations than classical stories and well-presented narratives about the real world.

We need to reconceive language arts as a school subject. In trying to make all students proficient readers and writers, there is no avoiding the responsibility of imparting the specific knowledge they will need to understand newspapers, magazines, and serious books directed at the national language community. There is no successful shortcut to teaching and learning this specific knowledge. Those who develop language arts programs at the school level or in publishing houses must understand that the skills they wish to impart are in fact knowledge-drenched and knowledge-constituted. The happy consequence will be reading programs that are much more absorbing, enjoyable, and interesting than the disjointed, pedestrian programs offered to students today.

5
USING SCHOOL TIME PRODUCTIVELY

TIME IS OF THE ESSENCE. Because of the Matthew effect, early opportunities for enhancing language comprehension, once wasted, may be lost permanently. What are the best ways to use school time productively, so we bring students from all social backgrounds to proficiency in reading and writing? How can we impart the most enabling language and knowledge as quickly as possible? Most reading activities that teachers and parents engage in with young children have been shown by research to be beneficial. But research rarely asks or answers a crucial question — what is the opportunity cost of engaging in this reading activity rather than that one?

"Opportunity cost" is an important concept from economics which reflects the fact that we forgo some benefits whenever we engage in one activity rather than another. If we read the same story three times to a child, we need to ask, how great are the benefits that the child will accrue by listening compared to the benefits if we had used that valuable time in more productive activities, such as reading other stories on the same topic? The principle of opportunity cost has become more important now that longer periods are being devoted to reading in school. New York City and California have ruled that 150 minutes — two and a half hours — of school time every day shall be spent on language arts in the early grades. Other states and localities require 90 minutes a day. This means that language arts are getting time that in the past may have been allotted to history, science, and the arts. Yet those neglected subjects are ultimately among the most essential ones for imparting reading skill.

Everyone knows that proficient reading requires an adequate vocabulary. Everyone also knows that children's vocabularies will get bigger when they hear or read stories. But not everyone knows how to answer these questions about time use: What is the most effective way to foster vocabulary gain? Is it better to read a child a short text of a different kind each day, or is it better to stay on a topic that stretches over several days or weeks? As we have seen, important research suggests that children can learn words much faster if we stick to the same topic for several sessions, because word learning occurs much faster — up to *four times faster* — when the verbal context is familiar.

Suppose, for example, you are reading to five-year-old Dmitri a story about kings and queens. If you extend that topic for the next few days by reading more true and fictional stories about kings and queens, how they lived, and what they did, the chances are that Dmitri will increase his general knowledge and vocabulary faster than if you read about zebras the next day, Laplanders the day after that, and so on. Clearly, then, a good way to induce fast vocabulary gain for young children (for whom so much is new and unfamiliar) is to stay on a subject long enough for the general topic to become familiar. This is yet another reason that a coherent, content-oriented curriculum is the most effective way to raise reading achievement.

Experts in the teaching of decoding skills have stated that time spent on decoding and encoding (writing) skills should not exceed thirty to forty-five minutes a day, so the bulk of classroom time is available for language and background knowledge.[1] What this means to you as a parent or a teacher of children in the earliest grades is that your children should simultaneously be receiving both explicit instruction in decoding and *coherent* instruction in the most enabling knowledge of language and the world. This double-pronged approach is the best way to advance reading proficiency.

As we have seen, international comparisons of reading achievement show that our schools are among the least productive in the developed world. Our children start school knowing on average as much as children in other developed nations, but each year that they stay in school they fall further behind. In grades three and four, U.S. performance is on a par with that of other developed countries. Then, in the middle-school grades, the differences grow, and the United States gradually drifts downward. In recent studies, our fourth-graders scored 42 points above the international normalized average of 500 — ninth in reading among thirty-five countries. By tenth grade they scored just 4 points above 500 — a decline of 38 normalized points between grade four and grade ten. They also exhibited a striking decline in relative ranking. Figure 1 shows this ski slope of reading achievement:[2]

A similar pattern is found in the most recent international studies of math. Our fourth-graders start out knowing approximately as

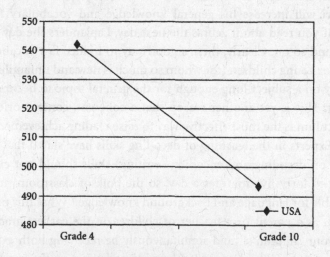

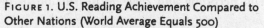

FIGURE 1. U.S. Reading Achievement Compared to Other Nations (World Average Equals 500)

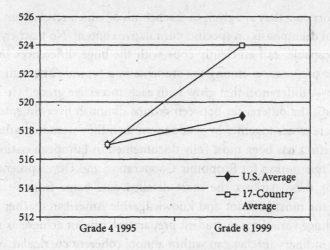

FIGURE 2. Math Achievement, Grade 4 to Grade 8

much reading and math as fourth-graders in other countries. By eighth grade, they have fallen behind those same students.[3]

It's possible, of course, that the reason for our relative decline with each successive grade lies in factors other than our unproductive use of school time — for instance, our distracting culture, our diversity, our racism, our unequal income distribution. But other developed nations have distracting cultures, ethnic diversity, racism, and unequal income distributions and nonetheless have higher-performing students. Sociological explanations are not very plausible when our school curricula and teaching methods are inherently unproductive. It is unnecessary to seek remote causes for our low educational productivity when more immediate ones are available.

BLAMING TEACHERS

Some people blame ineffective teachers for our poor showing over time on international comparisons. But so-called low teacher quality is not an innate characteristic of American teachers; it is the consequence of the training they have received and of the vague, incoherent curricula they are given to teach, both of which result from an ed school deemphasis on specific, cumulative content. No teacher, however capable, can efficiently cope with the huge differences in academic preparation among the students in a typical American classroom — differences that grow with each successive grade.[4] (In other nations, the differences between groups diminish over time, so that they are closer together by grade seven than they were in grade four. This effect has been most fully documented in European nations by the Organization for Economic Cooperation and Development, and among these nations, the most detailed data come from France.[5]) Even the most brilliant and knowledgeable American teacher faced with huge variations in student preparation cannot achieve as much as an ordinary teacher can within a more coherent curricular system like those found in the nations that outperform us.

The chief cause of our schools' inefficiency is precisely this curricular incoherence.[6] At the beginning of the school year, a teacher cannot be sure what the entering students know about a subject, because they have been taught very different topics in prior grades depending on the different preferences of their teachers. Typically, therefore, the teacher must spend a great deal of time at the beginning of each year in reviewing the preparatory material students need to know in order to learn the next topic — time that would not need to be so extensive (and so very boring to students who already have the knowledge) if he or she could be sure that the incoming students had all gained this knowledge already.[7]

Proposing to improve teacher quality without grasping the relationship between low teacher effectiveness and the romantic, formalistic ideas of the education world is to mistake an effect (teachers' inadequate subject-matter knowledge) for an underlying cause (the dominant ed-school ideas that withhold that knowledge from them). It is true that many American teachers are ill-informed about the subjects they teach, and it is also true that this reduces their productivity in the classroom. But this is not because of their inherent laziness or native incompetence. It is because they are subjected to antifact, how-to ideas during their training. American education schools consider it their job mainly to provide teachers with naturalistic and formalist ideologies. Teaching subject-matter knowledge in history, science, literature, and the arts (to the extent that it is considered to be needed at all) is an imprecisely defined task that education schools assign (without guidance) to the other departments of the college or university.[8] In short, the low productivity of our schools is chiefly caused by bad theory rather than by innate teacher incompetence. We will not improve teacher effectiveness until we change the unproductive romantic ideas that dominate teacher preparation and guarantee poor use of school time.

BETTER USE OF TIME LEADS TO GREATER FAIRNESS

An effective use of school time is especially important in all areas of learning connected with the advancement of language comprehension, which is inherently a slow process. For children who grow up in highly articulate homes, where they hear a wealth of language every day, the need to use time effectively in enlarging language comprehension is not as critical as it is for children who grow up in language-barren circumstances. Two researchers, Betty Hart and Todd Risley, have shown in detail how important the toddler years are for enhancing later understanding. Their pathbreaking work, in which many hours of speech interactions were recorded in the homes of very young children from different social groups, revealed that what toddlers heard at home in the way of speech patterns and vocabulary was hugely different depending on social class. Not only was the sheer quantity of words heard much less in some homes than in others, but also the styles of language use were vastly different. A child's ability to understand language turns out to be highly dependent on whether or not the parent says things like "Do you want to play with your chalk, or do you want to get your pegs out?" That's the kind of elaborated talk that middle-class toddlers hear. It is in contrast to the laconic utterances that tend to be used by less well educated parents, who say things like "Move!" and "Shut up!"[9]

Hart and Risley show that these differences in what very young children hear currently account for most of the variation in later reading progress. But it's important to stress that the *pattern* of this gap-widening result is an American pattern, which is different from the gap-closing effects of schooling in more productive school systems across the world. While it is true that disadvantaged students in those other developed nations never completely catch up in language skills, they do narrow the gap, as our students emphatically do not. One way of changing this result would be to change the habits and speech patterns of parents. As desirable as that might be, the speech differences between those in low-income and middle-class homes are likely to persist until our educational system improves over many years and educates future parents better. From the standpoint of progress in language right now, schools themselves should try to become supereffective middle-class homes. If we can do that, higher school achievement and greater equity will be the result.

When James Coleman, the great sociologist of education, analyzed the school characteristics that had the greatest impact on educational achievement and equity, he found that effective use of time was a chief factor. Most important was "intensity," a persistent, goal-directed focus on academics that caused classroom time to be used productively.[10] Schools with greater academic intensity produced not only greater learning but also greater equity. Such good schools not only raise achievement generally but also narrow the achievement gap between demographic groups. The first finding is obvious, since an intense focus on academics is self-evidently the most likely means to raise academic achievement. The second finding is more interesting, and it has positive implications for both advantaged and disadvantaged students.

The theoretical explanation for Coleman's finding about equity is this: when students learn more in school during the course of a classroom period and during an entire year, disadvantaged students begin to catch up — even when their advantaged peers are learning more or less the same things they are. That is because disadvantaged students start out knowing less, so each additional bit of learning is proportionally more enabling to them than to students who already knew more. If we are reading a story about Johnny Appleseed and some students know how plants grow while others don't, the latter group, the botanically challenged students, will be the ones who learn most from the story, although both groups will learn something new about Johnny Appleseed.

And there is a further reason for the equity effect that Coleman observed. When a lot of learning is going on in school, that fact changes the proportion between the academic knowledge gained in school and the academic knowledge gained outside school. When students are learning many academic things in the classroom, that will narrow the academic gap, because disadvantaged students are more dependent on schools for gaining academic information than advantaged students are. Advantaged students have a chance to learn a lot of academically relevant things from their homes and peer groups, whereas disadvantaged students learn academically relevant things mostly from their schools. Boosting the in-school proportion thus reduces the unfair distribution of out-of-school learning opportunities.

All of these considerations mean that a good school will be better for both advantaged and disadvantaged students. It will make a greater difference to disadvantaged students than to advantaged ones simply by virtue of being a good school. In a productive classroom, disadvantaged students are getting proportionally more out of schooling without holding back advantaged ones. On the other hand, if the school is an unproductive one, it will have a greater *negative* impact on disadvantaged than on advantaged students.[11] That is the reason American schools have not lived up to their democratic potential.

USING TIME EFFECTIVELY

The most productive way to impart reading proficiency to children is to build up the most enabling linguistic and world knowledge cumulatively in the most time-effective way. When children are offered coherent, cumulative knowledge from preschool on, they become good readers. A coherent approach to content will produce this result even in the absence of a good, content-oriented language arts program, as the results in Core Knowledge schools show.[12] These are American schools that follow a detailed, grade-by-grade topic sequence that my colleagues and I have worked out and field-tested over the past fifteen years, similar in structure to the sequence followed in high-performing systems in Europe and Asia.[13] If students in these schools were offered not just this coherent sequence in history, the arts, literature, math, and science but also a content-oriented language arts program, integrated with the curriculum as a whole, their already superior progress in reading would become even more rapid.

The fullest evidence for the validity of this prediction comes from large-scale studies conducted by French researchers into the effects of very early knowledge instruction in school on later reading achievement.[14] The French are in a good position to perform such studies. They have been running state-sponsored preschools for more than a hundred years. By age five, almost 100 percent of French children, including the children of immigrants from Africa, Asia, and southern Europe, attend preschools. At age four, 85 percent of all children attend, and astonishingly, at age two, 30 percent of all children attend. Analyses of records from tens of thousands of students — records that include detailed information about race, ethnicity, and social class — show that the earlier the child starts, the greater the positive effect on reading will be. By the end of fifth grade in France, the relative benefit to disadvantaged pupils who start at the amazingly early age of two rather than four is over one half of a standard deviation, quite a large effect. Those who start at age three do better in later reading than those who start at age four, and starting school at age four is better than starting at age five. These studies show that the long-term gain in starting early is greater for disadvantaged than for advantaged students, thus confirming the theory that effective schooling is in itself compensatory.[15]

But because progress in language is slow, the relative academic benefits revealed by these French data do not show up fully until grade five and beyond. This delayed effect is a very important and understudied feature of good early schooling. A deferred effect similar to that found in the large-scale French studies was also found in an analysis by F. D. Smith of the reading scores in a Core Knowledge school compared with those of a control school.[16] In that longitudinal study, the students in the Core Knowledge school received the Core Knowledge curriculum, a coherent, grade-by-grade curriculum designed to provide them with the knowledge most useful for reading comprehension. The students in the control school received the standard how-to, hands-on curriculum that prevails in most schools throughout the nation. In kindergarten through grade three, test scores of both groups of students were on a par. In fact, the Core Knowledge students were somewhat behind. But by grade six there was a large differential effect favoring the Core Knowledge students, both in reading achievement and in equity. Figure 3 on the next page shows the achievement effect.

Some of the explanation for these patterns of deferred effects can be found in the work of Joseph Torgesen and his colleagues, who showed that reading tests vary in their emphases as students advance through the elementary grades.[17] In the earliest grades, scores on standard reading tests depend most on mastering the mechanics of reading — on being fluent and accurate in the decoding of words. Thus in the earliest grades, scores on standard reading tests are relatively less dependent on students' world and word knowledge. With each advancing grade, because of the changing nature of the tests, the factors that are most important for test scores change. In later grades,

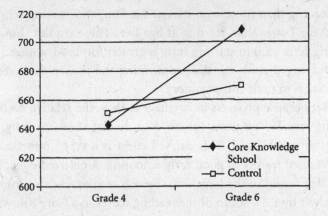

FIGURE 3. Stanford 9 Reading Scores, Grade 4 to Grade 6,
Core Knowledge School Compared to Control School

reading scores depend most on word and world knowledge.[18] This means that even if parents and teachers are doing everything they should to use time effectively in the early grades, they can't expect immediate, large improvements in reading comprehension. But they are laying essential groundwork. The data show that the improvements will indeed show up later.

6

USING TESTS PRODUCTIVELY

ARE TESTS DRIVING OUR SCHOOLS?

NO EFFORT TO REFORM and improve our schools, such as this book proposes, can ignore testing, which currently determines what states, schools, teachers, and students do. In order to receive full benefits from the federal government, schools are required to show adequate yearly progress on reading tests for all social groups. Americans should support this stipulation of the No Child Left Behind law — which has proved difficult to meet — as it is a praiseworthy inducement to fairness and accountability. Tests of academic progress are the only practical way to hold schools accountable for educating all children and are therefore essential to the twin aims of quality and fairness. Administrators who have not met the requirement often claim that lack of federal money is the reason, but we might have expected the states, with or without a federal law, to be concerned with whether children are making adequate progress each year. Finding out through standardized tests is not expensive. Making and giving tests is not a big part of a state's educational budget.

A teacher once told me that she hated standardized tests. When I asked her, "Would you think they were so bad if your students aced them?" she said, "No, then I'd love them." The remark is far from cynical. A teacher (and her students) *should* love to find out that they are making real progress. Many of the complaints against the No Child

Left Behind law pertain to the supposedly harmful influence of intensive preparation for the standardized reading tests. Yes, the prepping (as conducted) is harmful! But a variety of other complaints against reading tests are not justified — that they distort education, or that there is an overemphasis on tests and accountability. These objections seem justified only because there is a lack of fit between the kind of education that promotes significant progress in reading and the kind of education that the schools have currently devised in their unsuccessful attempts to raise scores on reading tests. If the schools understood how to bring all students to reading proficiency, they would certainly do so. Many of the complaints against the tests and even the need to prepare for them would then disappear.

States are now obliged to test children in reading at every grade level, starting in third grade, in order to receive NCLB benefits. Before the law was passed, they did not have admirable accountability requirements. Some states gave tests only every third or fourth year, which was problematic, since each new school year brings the child a new teacher, who needs to know where the students stand. When I taught practicing teachers in an education school in a state that required tests only every third year, they told me that few teachers wanted to teach in the grades in which the children were to be tested, because, as they rightly surmised, they would be blamed for the faults of their predecessors in prior grades. Yearly testing is essential both to keep track of each student's progress and to encourage teachers to cooperate in providing students with a coherent education in which each grade can build on the previous one.

I want to outline some facts about reading tests that are not widely known yet need to be familiar to any parent, teacher, or citizen who is interested in educational improvement. I will cut through some of the jargon surrounding testing, and I will show how we can use standardized tests of reading to foster a rich and formative education that will meet the requirements of adequate yearly progress for all groups with flying colors.

THE FLAWS OF STATE TESTS

Here are fourth-grade guidelines for teaching and testing reading comprehension, as published by three representative states (all states issue these kinds of guidelines).

Texas

Reading/comprehension. The student comprehends selections using a variety of strategies. The student is expected to:

(A) use his/her own knowledge and experience to comprehend;

(B) establish and adjust purposes for reading such as reading to find out, to understand, to interpret, to enjoy, and to solve problems;

(C) monitor his/her own comprehension and make modifications when understanding breaks down such as by re-reading a portion aloud, using reference aids, searching for clues, and asking questions;

(D) describe mental images that text descriptions evoke;

(E) use the text's structure or progression of ideas such as cause and effect or chronology to locate and recall information;

(F) determine a text's main (or major) ideas and how those ideas are supported with details;

(G) paraphrase and summarize text to recall, inform, and organize ideas;

(H) draw inferences such as conclusions or generalizations and support them with text evidence and experience.

New York

Students will listen, speak, read, and write for information and understanding. As listeners and readers, students will collect data, facts, and ideas; discover relationships, concepts, and generalizations; and use knowledge generated from oral, written, and electronically produced texts.

- interpret and analyze information from textbooks and nonfiction books for young adults, as well as reference materials, audio and media presentations, oral interviews, graphs, charts, diagrams, and electronic databases intended for a general audience
- compare and synthesize information from different sources
- use a wide variety of strategies for selecting, organizing, and categorizing information
- distinguish between relevant and irrelevant information and between fact and opinion
- relate new information to prior knowledge and experience
- understand and use the text features that make information accessible and usable, such as format, sequence, level of diction, and relevance of details.

Florida

The student constructs meaning from a wide range of texts.

1. reads text and determines the main idea or essential message, identifies relevant supporting details and facts, and arranges events in chronological order.
2. identifies the author's purpose in a simple text.
3. recognizes when a text is primarily intended to persuade.
4. identifies specific personal preferences relative to fiction and nonfiction reading.
5. reads and organizes information for a variety of purposes, including making a report, conducting interviews, taking a test, and performing an authentic task.
6. recognizes the difference between fact and opinion presented in a text.

Given such guidelines, consider the Kafkaesque predicament of schools and students under the current accountability arrangements. *The tests are coming! We don't know what topics the children will be asked to read about. The tests will probe reading comprehension skills, so we must teach those skills!*

Here are some examples of questions that appear in the fourth-grade tests put out by these states. As you will see, all of them dutifully follow the criterion that the student should be able to identify the main idea.

Texas

Paragraph 4 is mainly about

how hard it is to become a *mahout*
how elephants move trees
how the *mahouts* control the elephants
how *mahouts* protect the sanctuary

New York

This article is mostly about

how the Appalachian Trail came to exist
when people can visit the Appalachian Trail
who hikes the most on the Appalachian Trail
why people work together on the Appalachian Trail

Florida

Which detail supports the author's main idea?

Orcas ruin his fishing profits
Killer whales travel in pods
Orcas prey in the ocean depths
Killer whales are intelligent

How does one prepare students to take this kind of test? The schools have decided, on the advice of experts, that they must train students in the kinds of procedures elicited by the test: Clarify what the passage means. Question the author. Find the main idea. Make inferences about the passage. Study the meanings of words. Consider which event in the narrative comes first, and which next — all the sorts of deadening exercises that Linda Perlstein observed in her report. I call the situation Kafkaesque because, like characters in Kafka, the students and teachers are doing all the things they are supposed to do, and yet after the scores are totted up, despite their dutiful efforts, they have not fulfilled the mysterious requirements demanded by the authorities: reading scores have not improved significantly. That is because the tests are not testing comprehension *strategies,* as the states and test-makers suppose. They are testing *comprehension,* which is a different matter altogether. Reading comprehension is emphatically not a universal, repeatable skill like sounding out words or throwing a ball through a hoop. General reading comprehension is a simplified conception for something complex. It is an abstraction that stands for a whole array of separate, content-constituted skills, like the skill of reading about the Appalachian Mountains or the skill of reading about the Civil War. Unlike formal decoding skill, proficiency in one reading comprehension task does not necessarily predict skill in another.[1]

THE NATURE OF READING TESTS

As we have seen, a student's actual ability to find the main idea of a passage is not a formal ability to follow procedures that will elicit the main idea but the ability to understand what the text says. Let's look at a characteristic bit of prose from one of these reading tests.

> There is a path that starts in Maine and ends in Georgia, 2,167 miles later. This path is called the Appalachian Trail. If you want, you can walk the whole way, although only some people who try to do this actually make it, because it is so far, and they get tired. The idea for the trail came from a man named Benton MacKaye. In 1921 he wrote an article about how people needed a nearby place where they could enjoy nature and take a break from work. He thought the Appalachian Mountains would be perfect for this.

No repetitions of classroom exercises will help the test-taker who does not know what hiking is, or what low, tree-covered mountains are like (they are not like the snow-covered Himalaya-type mountains most often pictured in books), or where Maine and Georgia are. Classroom practice in strategies cannot make up for the student's lack of the background knowledge needed to understand this passage, and no instruction in strategies is required to answer the questions quickly and accurately if the student knows about hiking, the Appalachians, Maine, and Georgia. The inferences that we make when we hear or read speech are based on a situation model particular to that utterance, derived from relevant knowledge about the domain of the passage. The comprehension skills that students are supposed to learn by practicing "comprehension skills" cannot lead to high test performance, because they do not lead to actual comprehension. If students really could gain isolated "inferencing" abilities from their strategy exercises, they would not be in their Kafkaesque trap.

In principle, there is nothing wrong with the format of most state reading tests as measures of general reading ability. But because the tests have been presented as tests of formal comprehension skills, they are unwittingly unfair, because these skills are not what they are really testing. The tests favor children who happen to have domain knowledge relevant to the passages in the test. Many test-makers go to some lengths to provide the background knowledge that they believe is needed within the tests themselves. They supply pictures. They define key words before the passage starts. But these efforts do not succeed in leveling the playing field, because students who are unfamiliar with a text's subject matter are slowed down by assimilating and applying the new background information before they consciously apply strategies to try to figure out the right answer.

Conscious strategizing is slow and cumbersome. Moreover, as we have seen, it takes the mind much longer to process meanings of a text on an unfamiliar topic. Speed is slower and scores are lower for unfamiliar topics than for familiar ones. This is true for all readers.[2] Tests are time-sensitive, as reading comprehension itself is, because slowness implies mental overload, and mental overload impairs understanding. The mental speed that is bestowed by topic familiarity is important not just for completing the test on time but also for getting the answers right. In sum, a child who already knows about the Appalachian Trail, who has heard or read about it or seen or walked on or read about similar trails, will process the passage much faster and more accurately than a child to whom such things are unfamiliar, even though the two children have identical decoding and strategizing skills. They are equally smart. They have learned equally well the lessons that the classroom has taught. Yet these two students make vastly different scores on the reading test, because one student possesses more general knowledge than the other.

There are various ways of looking at the unfairness that results when two children who have the same school-taught strategy skills receive very different scores on a reading test. Some have argued that these supposedly neutral tests are culturally biased, which is certainly true. While the test-makers attempt to be fair by making the tests knowledge-neutral, they do not succeed in this aim. Language comprehension can never be knowledge-neutral. A more accurate way of perceiving the inherent unfairness of these tests is to concede that although they cannot possibly be knowledge-neutral and therefore fair to students who don't have the needed knowledge, they are perfectly appropriate as tests of reading ability. That is, their unfairness resides in the pretense that formal reading skills are being tested when in fact relevant background knowledge is being tested. Ultimately, the unfairness resides in the failure of schools to impart to all children the background knowledge they need to understand the passages on the test and similar passages in real life.

The lack of connection between the knowledge-constituted character of reading and the skills pretense of the state tests is glossed over in the technical jargon of testing, which amply confuses the general public as well as many educators. One of the main examples is the technical distinction between "norm-referenced" and "criterion-referenced" tests. The state tests from which I just extracted some main-idea items are criterion-referenced, because students in Texas, New York, and Florida are not to be measured against each other on a percentile scale, as happens with norm-referenced tests; they are to be measured against a definite criterion, namely, whether they have achieved the learning goals set forth in the state guidelines for the fourth grade. They either do or don't meet the specified standard. So instead of being scored in percentiles, they are scored according to a standard of acceptability or nonacceptability, such as "proficient" and "below proficient." The point that lies between "proficient" and "below proficient" is labeled the "cut score." This characteristic of criterion-referenced tests supposedly makes them fair and educationally productive, since everyone knows the criterion and in theory can study for it. The schools are supposed to teach to the criterion and the tests to test it.

But recall what the state criteria are: "draw inferences such as conclusions or generalizations," "determine a text's main (or major) ideas." On these empty standards, any reading test, past or present (including any norm-referenced test, as I shall show in a moment), could be considered a criterion-referenced test. Any passage on the test and its accompanying questions would fulfill the criterion as long as they include items asking the student to find the main idea and so on, *and all reading tests do this.* Thus, in the case of reading, the phrase "criterion-referenced," suggesting that the state tests are somehow based on the curriculum in a meaningful way, is very misleading. Texas reading tests would automatically meet Michigan criteria and vice versa; Florida reading tests could be used in New York and automatically meet its criteria. Why not? The state standards for reading comprehension describe empty processes. These abstract, knowledge-evasive criteria do not reflect the knowledge-based character of reading comprehension. Even if these tests were valid and reliable (an issue somewhat in doubt), they would still be inadequate when conceived as criterion-referenced tests that could productively guide schooling.[3]

Given the unfair variations in scoring from one state to another as well as the variations in the quality of state reading tests, it is worth taking a look at the makeup of well-established norm-referenced tests of reading, such as the California Test of Basic Skills (CTBS), the Stanford 9, the Gates-MacGinitie Reading Tests, the Iowa Test of Basic Skills (ITBS), and others.[4] These tests can be (and have been) used as criterion-referenced tests of reading comprehension simply by using students' actual scores instead of their percentile standings. Unlike the state tests, whose comparability with other tests is largely unknown, these standardized tests have been refined technically for many years and yield similar results when compared with one another. In reading comprehension they exhibit a correlation coefficient of around .8, and the correlations are even higher in the middle range of scores comprising 75 percent of students — around .9.[5] These high intertest correlations show that they are highly reliable — that is, they yield similar results with similar populations of test-takers. They have also been determined to be valid as measures of reading ability. (Validity means they really do measure what they claim to measure, and reliability means the scores are consistently similar with similar populations.) Their consistency has been measured carefully and at great expense. Their accuracy in measuring real-world abilities has been determined from their high correlation with a number of real-world competencies. For example, test scores in early grades predict scores in later years. Scores predict school grades. Scores predict job performance and income.[6]

If we compare the reading comprehension sections of these nationwide tests with the reading comprehension sections of the less well calibrated state tests, we find that though the tests are called by different names, they are structurally the same. The individual student's scores on any state test could be reported in percentiles, just as her scores on any percentile-reported test could be reported as being above or below a determined cut score. None of this reporting activity would change the actual score or the underlying nature of the test.

What are these tests like? Let's look at the fourth-grade reading comprehension section of one of these standard tests — the ITBS. It contains nine short passages of different genres: fiction about a bird, a biography, some lyric poetry, fiction about sports, exposition about another country, fiction about a TV program, exposition about the habits of an animal, exposition about the lives of Native Americans, exposition about a religious sect. The prose passages are short — 150 to 290 words — and each is followed by around four multiple-choice questions. Now let's look at the reading comprehension component of a highly regarded state test, the FCAT of Florida. The test items have very similar characteristics — ten short, heterogeneous passages, each followed by multiple-choice questions similar to those on the ITBS. The ITBS probably has some technical advantages, owing to its continued refinement over many years, but it is very likely that the FCAT and the ITBS will yield similar results in reading comprehension. Structurally, they are the same.

Every highly valid and reliable reading test contains several different passages sampling several knowledge areas and kinds of writing. That fact in itself gives away the knowledge-based character of reading, since if reading comprehension were a set of all-purpose formal strategies, a single passage would test reading skill perfectly well. But because general reading skill requires broad general knowledge, a valid test must sample several genres and areas of knowledge. Because of this sampling requirement, there will be no structural difference between well-designed state or national tests of reading comprehension. In short, there is no inherent difference between criterion-referenced and norm-referenced reading tests. Standardized tests like ITBS are inherently criterion-referenced, if we regard the criterion as "general reading comprehension ability." The several domains on a valid reading test are chosen not because they directly reflect what is taught in school but because they reflect an ability to read passages from an unpredictable diversity of domains. In order to read a wide array of passages in different domains, a person must have a wide array of knowledge. This is a key point, and it is currently missed in conceptualizing these tests and the instruction to prepare for them.[7]

WHAT KINDS OF TESTS WILL ENHANCE EDUCATION?

How can we calm the frantic and ineffectual test preparations of the schools and enable them to meet the adequate-yearly-progress requirement much more readily? Students and teachers cannot directly prepare for a reading test. No one should be able to predict the subject matter of the passages on such a test and specifically learn about it. That would be cheating. It would defeat the test's purpose, which is to discover how well the test-taker can be expected to read an unpredictable array of texts in and out of school. The essence of such a test is its unpredictability. But if you cannot predict a valid reading test, how can you prepare for it? You can't, and therefore you shouldn't try. You should prepare for a reading test *indirectly*, by becoming a good reader of a broad range of texts — an ability that requires broad general knowledge.

The standard reading comprehension tests, then, though adequate as reading tests, have severe shortcomings when used to measure yearly student progress in the early grades. Their two most damaging flaws are, first, that they do not positively influence instruction, since they are unrelated to any content curriculum, and second, that they cannot accurately measure yearly progress. Standard reading tests are not appropriate for fine-scale diagnoses of the precise areas of a student's deficiencies, nor are they reliable guides to the curriculum that students should be receiving to improve their background knowledge for reading. In the early grades especially, when children are making irregular, desultory progress in knowledge and vocabulary that cannot be sensitively measured by such tests, general reading tests are quite inadequate gauges.

Like all tests, a reading comprehension test is a sampling device. It doesn't test the whole range of possible knowledge domains or kinds of text. That would make it far too long. It offers a few typical samples from a few typical domains, and students' performance on these samples is taken to predict their reading comprehension over the whole universe of reading tasks that confront the general reader. The best of the tests do a very good job of making that prediction. Although imparting the general knowledge needed for general reading ability is a multiyear project, covering at least the first six years of schooling and beyond, real progress in reading comprehension can occur in the early grades without sampling that knowledge on a reading test. If a student has just learned about the Civil War, he may not make a noticeably better grade on a short reading test that samples domains far removed from that subject. But he will nonetheless be able to read passages about Grant and Lee and Lincoln with more comprehension than he did before, even if the test does not measure that progress. He will also be able to read about events related to war and history with greater comprehension. He will know what a regiment is and what the word *bloodshed* means, though these are not on the test. He may have learned more about some of the words on the test and still not be able to answer correctly, because some of his gradual gains in word understanding, a slow, subliminal process requiring many exposures to a word, do not reach the measurement threshold of the test.

Let me quickly say that this is not an attack on these tests, and especially not on the best of them, like the ITBS. In fact, it would be sound policy to use these more established and reliable tests to measure reading ability instead of those currently made and used by the states. My real point is more radical, and, I hope, more interesting than simply criticizing tests, which are inherently necessary in education. If schools wish to meet the adequate-yearly-progress requirement, they should *systematically teach and then test for the general knowledge that leads to proficient reading comprehension.* The monitors of NCLB compliance should recognize that adequate yearly progress in early reading is in fact occurring if students show that they are not only decoding well but also gaining general knowledge, as demonstrated on curriculum-based tests of specific knowledge rather than simply on reading tests. Behind the current conception of reading, measurable, linear progress seems to be assumed. That is a reasonably correct model for the repeated, mechanical aspects of reading, such as decoding. (One of the best measures of decoding skill is the ability to sound out combinations of letters that don't have any meaning at all.) But adequate yearly progress in reading comprehension cannot be accurately measured in early grades by these current tests, because much relevant learning is still latent, and the tests do not necessarily sample the knowledge areas in which progress in comprehension may have occurred.

This analysis suggests that there are far better indications of adequate yearly progress in early schooling than general reading tests that have no direct connection with the content of the school curriculum. In the early grades especially, reading tests cannot be highly sensitive measures of adequate progress in school. They are not designed to measure progress in schooling; they are designed to measure general reading ability from a sampling of subject matter that may not correspond directly to the schooling that has been provided during the year. There is a lack of fit between what needs to be taught and what is being measured.

The key to an improved test policy is to continue to use tests like ITBS and CTBS at the end of the year, as partial indicators of progress in general reading ability, especially in decoding, but to supplement them with *curriculum-based tests* that determine how well students have learned the well-defined content of the year's curriculum in all subjects. We need this second kind of test to measure adequate yearly progress accurately and sensitively. Such tests would be truly criterion-based, in fact as well as in name. And they would have a powerfully beneficial effect on reading ability and on education in general. This mode of testing will encourage students and schools to learn the words and things that over time lead to reading proficiency, and at the same time it will insure that students get proper credit for what they have actually learned and the progress they have actually made. Such knowledge-based tests are also needed to encourage and insure long-range improvement in reading comprehension, which, as we have shown, is a skill that depends on students acquiring a wide range of general knowledge.

These content tests should be specifically tied to the knowledge goals of a sound education in literature, science, history, and the arts, for these are the large domains that constitute the background knowledge required for reading comprehension. Ideally, the curricula to which the tests are tied should be focused on the knowledge that is most important and enabling from the standpoint of later learning and reading ability. It takes several years of systematic, cumulative learning before schoolchildren can gain the general knowledge and conceptual fluency they need to be good readers. To those who might object that I am recommending more rather than less testing, I reply that content testing leads to engaging, productive, and interesting teaching, whereas drill-and-kill process testing does not.

John Bishop, of Cornell University, has shown that educational systems which require definite content standards *and* use curriculum-based content tests to determine whether the curriculum has been learned greatly improve achievement for all students, including those from less advantaged backgrounds.[8] Additional evidence in support of curriculum-based content testing comes from the recent finding that gains in reading are directly proportional to the completeness with which a school implements a coherent, content-rich curriculum.[9] A system of specific content standards coupled with curriculum-based tests will cause achievement on *non*-curriculum-based tests to rise over time. It will result in higher achievement overall and a narrowing of the academic gap between rich and poor.

We should abandon the formalistic conception behind current testing policy in reading comprehension. It is a self-defeating policy based on mistaken ideas, and it should be replaced by a testing policy that encourages schools to teach the general knowledge that will lead to proficient reading comprehension. Breadth of knowledge is the single factor within human control that contributes most to academic achievement and general cognitive competence. In contradiction to the theory of social determinism, breadth of knowledge is a far greater factor in achievement than socioeconomic status. The positive correlation between achieved ability and socioeconomic status is only half the correlation between achieved ability and the possession of general information. That is to say, being "smart" is more dependent on possessing general knowledge than on family background per se.[10] This little-known and quite momentous fact means that imparting broad knowledge to all children is the single most effective way to narrow the competence gap between demographic groups through schooling. The tests we give should reflect our understanding of this truth.

7

ACHIEVING COMMONALITY
AND FAIRNESS

READING AND A WIDER CRISIS

UNTIL WE SOLVE the reading problem, we can neither compete optimally in the knowledge economy nor fulfill the aim of giving every child a fair start in life. In solving the reading problem, more is at stake even than economic prosperity and fairness. The very fabric of our peaceable and unified democracy is at risk when we do not know how to communicate with each other. Reading comprehension depends on the more primordial understanding of speech that occurs within the common public sphere, on the shared knowledge that enables verbal comprehension in general. A content-neutral, skills-oriented concept of education has the unintended effect of depressing reading scores and diminishing the shared content we need for communication and solidarity within the nation as a whole. The red-state/blue-state phenomenon is just one sign of this decline of commonality. Lack of communication between generations and a general lack of trust between groups are others. People who cannot communicate well with one another do not trust one another. They do not feel a sense of responsibility to the larger community. A lot is being written about the culture wars in the United States. Such conflict is inevitable in a big, diverse country. But some of the polarization has less to do with ideology than with the inherent suspicion and lack of solidarity among people who fail to share a common basis of knowledge — a commonality of discourse that alone enables shared allusion and mutual comprehension.

The practical focus of this book on improving reading comprehension is therefore a way into larger, more portentous issues. Reading scores would be greatly improved if we offered students a cumulative content-oriented reading program during the class periods devoted to language arts. But that remedy, if left by itself, would be a less than optimal solution. As we have seen, high reading skill is the result of a good general early education, not of a narrow emphasis on reading as such. A focus on the ninety minutes currently being devoted to language arts each day is a practical beginning. But a knowledge orientation to language arts by itself will not change the skills orientation of our schools. We need to supplement that with a knowledge approach to *all* school subjects.

FULFILLING OUR NATION'S HIGHEST IDEALS

The American principle of opportunity and fairness implies not just effective early education but also a degree of commonality in education. The founders of our educational principles, Thomas Jefferson in Virginia and, later, Horace Mann in Massachusetts, saw this implication clearly as the very essence of the democratic ideal. The child of the prince and the child of the pauper deserve the same initial chance. These founders did not propose giving all children merely the same *kind* of initial chance, but rather an *identical* early education. They reasoned that in a democracy, we can't predict who will end up as a pauper and who as a president. Jefferson therefore proposed giving children an identical early education at state expense. Massachusetts actually instituted what Jefferson had proposed — the "common school."

In offering a common curriculum, Horace Mann recognized another value besides equality of opportunity. He believed that such a curriculum not only gives everyone an equal chance, it also enables everyone to participate in the public sphere. According to Mann, an important reason for offering the same early education to all children was not only to bring them into the democracy and economy of the nation but to encourage national solidarity and community. Commonality of knowledge, he thought, would expand people's sympathies beyond their narrow group interests to embrace the interests of the nation as a whole. Here is how he stated that perceptive insight, in the famous twelfth report of the Massachusetts school board in 1848:

> A fellow-feeling for one's class or caste is the common instinct of hearts not wholly sunk in selfish regards for person, or for family. The spread of education, by enlarging the cultivated class or caste, will open a wider area over which the social feelings will expand; and, if this education should be universal and complete, it would do more than all things else to obliterate factitious distinctions in society.

Mann understood that fairness and social solidarity alike are linked to the common school. The two aims go together. You cannot have good early education that is fair to all without a common body of content, and without a common body of content, you cannot have national solidarity. Yet common content is the one thing that is made impossible by the reigning ideas and practices of our schools. It is no wonder that we are failing both in education and in solidarity.

CONSTANTLY CHANGING SCHOOLS — A CRITICAL ISSUE

Mobility is a misleading term to denote students' moving from one school to another in the middle of the year. The percentage of economically disadvantaged students who migrate during the school year is appallingly high, and the effects are dishearteningly severe. One study has analyzed those effects on 9,915 children. With this large group, the researchers were able to factor out the influences of poverty, race, single-parent status, and lack of parental education in order to isolate just the effects of changing schools. Even with other adverse influences factored out, children who changed schools often were much more likely than those who did not to exhibit behavioral problems and to fail a grade.[1] The researchers found that the adverse effects of such social and academic incoherence are greatly intensified when parents have low educational levels and when compensatory education is not available in the home. But this big fact of student mobility is generally ignored in discussions of school reform. It is as if that elephant in the middle of the parlor is less relevant or important than other concerns, such as the supposed dangers of encouraging uniformity or of allowing an "outsider" to decide what subjects are to be taught at which grade level.

The finding that our mobile students (who are preponderantly from low-income families) perform worse than stable ones does not mean that their lower performance is a consequence of poverty. That is to commit the fallacy of social determinism. Where there is greater commonality of the curriculum, the effects of mobility are less severe. In a summary of research on student mobility, Herbert Walberg states that "common learning goals, curriculum, and assessment within states (or within an entire nation) . . . alleviate the grave learning disabilities faced by children, especially poorly achieving children, who move from one district to another with different curricula, assessment, and goals."[2] The adverse effects of student mobility are much less severe in countries that use a nationwide core curriculum than in the United States, where no national guidelines alleviate the trauma and incoherence of the fragmented educational experience of the millions of students who change schools in the middle of the year.

The United States has the highest school mobility rate of all developed countries. The statistics are eloquent, and need to be stated and restated rather than ignored. According to the most recent census, every year 45 percent of Americans change their residence.[3] Among these domestic migrants are over 20 million schoolchildren between the ages of five and fourteen. Those in the lowest income brackets move most frequently. Few caregivers are able to time their moves to coincide with the beginning and end of the school year. Not all of these changes of residence by children entail changes of their school, but a large percentage of them do.[4] In a typical American school district, the average rate at which students transfer in and out of schools during the academic year is about one third.[5] In a typical inner-city school, only about half the students who start in September are still there in May — a mobility rate of 50 percent.[6] The General Accounting Office reports that one sixth of all third-graders attend at least three schools between first and third grade. A quarter of low-income third-graders have attended at least three different schools. Among students with limited English proficiency, 34 percent of third-graders have attended three schools.[7] A much larger percentage of these migrating third-graders read below grade level, as compared to those who have not yet changed schools.[8] The average mobility rates for the inner city lie routinely between 45 percent and 80 percent, with many suburban rates between 25 percent and 40 percent. Some schools in New York and other cities have mobility rates of over 100 percent — that is, the total number of students moving in and out during the year exceeds the total number of students attending the school.[9]

Given the curricular incoherence in a typical American school even for those who stay at the same school, the education provided to frequently moving students is tragically fragmented. The high mobility of low-income parents guarantees that disadvantaged children will be most severely affected by the educational handicaps of changing schools, and that they will be the ones who are most adversely affected by lack of commonality across schools. In an earlier book I deplored the "myth of the local curriculum" — a myth because lack of commonality across classrooms in the same school and across schools in the same district means that no definable curriculum exists.[10] I should have added to this the "myth of the local school." The term *local school* implies a thereness, a stability. But if our idea of school includes, as it should, not just the building and the staff but also the students who attend it during the year, then the notion of a local school begins to fade into something that shifts like sand dunes. If we include students in our concept, then there are relatively few local schools in any stable sense in the urban United States, and almost none that are attended chiefly by disadvantaged students.

LOCALISM AND A PERFECT STORM OF BAD EDUCATIONAL IDEAS

Along with the terrible trinity of naturalism, formalism, and determinism, localism deserves a dishonored place in American education. Among the wider public it may be the most powerful educational idea of all. Localism has less to do with educational arguments than with American traditions. On the surface, it simply implies that our state or our town will decide what shall be taught in our schools. It says nothing about what those things should be, so localism is another content-free idea, and as a practical matter it powerfully reinforces an approach that is short on content. It brings liberals and conservatives together to collaborate in support of anticontent, process-oriented ideas about education.

Liberals and conservatives alike are suspicious of imposed content. Conservatives want local citizens rather than the state to decide what should be taught. They fear that a government curriculum would force-feed children "abominations" like *Heather Has Two Mommies.* Liberals fear that a government curriculum would force-feed children things like Christian theology and anti-Darwinism. Both groups worry that if decisions on curriculum are taken away from towns and states, the other side will impose its repugnant ideological views on schooling. Localism encourages the process curriculum as the safe ground on which liberals and conservatives can meet. After all, if there is no definitely imposed content, there is nothing to object to.

This suspicion-fed collaboration between liberals and conservatives helps explain why the process point of view has persisted despite its inability to raise achievement or attain fairness. Educationist, process ideas thrive on the liberal-conservative standoff, and our schools and school boards operate under a gentlemen's agreement that unites these groups behind the process-oriented creed. An undefined local curriculum that is free of specifically ordained content cannot be inherently liberal or conservative. However, a process-oriented curriculum cannot be educationally effective, either. That is the devil's pact that is being made in American education.

The federal government does not set curricula in the United States. Under the tradition of localism, individual districts have, until the very recent "standards movement," set out their own guidelines, which have been remarkably vague.[11] Now the states are beginning to influence the content of the school curriculum, although as many observers have pointed out, current state standards are usually just as unspecific as the vague, process-oriented district curricula. Typically, state standards in language arts do not mention a single required text and thereby avoid giving offence to any group. But is there evidence that if a state did decide to provide a detailed, grade-by-grade specification of core content, it would use that content as an instrument of indoctrination, as both liberals and conservatives fear?

The public schools in a democracy should not take sides in still-disputed areas. Gay marriage comes to mind. Children are required to attend school. They must not be compelled to attend a school that inculcates ideas that their parents and caregivers find repugnant. The United States, because of its history of religious refuge, has a first-rate tradition of cultural sensitivity — for example, in the way it has treated Amish beliefs and sensibilities. Unlike the French, with their powerfully secular traditions, we do not and would not forbid Muslim girls to wear headscarves. It is true that the absolute claims of religion constantly press against American secular political traditions. But a basic theme of American history is that the common public sphere is tolerant and allows each sect to interact with others under the umbrella of secular law, so long as it does not impose on others. Deeply inbred in our history and law is the principle that this tolerant civil polity will trump each intolerant sect that tries to control other sects or antisects. When the Board of Education of Kansas, populated by religious conservatives, seemed to overstep that principle of keeping controversial issues out of the schools, public opinion compelled it to retreat.

A subtler point is that the very act of defining very *openly* what should be taught in school would be a better protection against illegitimate mind control than the current vague, process-oriented guidelines. A highly public and open specification of what core subject matter will be taught, grade by grade, is a much safer protection against indoctrination in the public schools than the current arrangement, under which nobody really knows what is being taught.

Currently, the main sources of indoctrination are teachers, not textbooks. Textbook publishers, wishing to sell in every state, are careful to exclude what might be offensive under the cover of a how-to approach to education.[12] But this orientation, in which content is not specified, actually invites indoctrination at the hands of the teacher. Under the covering idea that what counts is how-to knowledge, and in the absence of specific content guidelines, the teacher is left free to teach critical thinking and deep understanding with whatever content seems appropriate. I well remember picking up a German grammar book in Communist East Berlin long before the Berlin wall was erected. Precisely because the book was oriented to the formal elements of German grammar, the content was left to the indoctrinators. If the grammar was to teach declarative sentences, examples were sentences like "The American capitalist imperialist is unfair to the worker." The formal character of an imperative sentence was shown in "Yankee, go home!" A process orientation offers no inherent protection against indoctrination. Irresponsibility is much less likely to occur when the schools are clear about the basic specific academic content that children should be taught at a particular grade level.

Are There Decisive Advantages in Specifying Definite Content?

The aim of imparting high reading ability to children has turned out to entail imparting broad knowledge to them. This in turn requires us to oversee some of the content that will be taught at each grade level, in order to avoid the huge gaps and boring repetitions that currently characterize the schooling many children receive. An excellent account of the surprising fact that a public school curriculum typically does not actually exist in the United States is Roger Shattuck's recent piece in the *New York Review of Books* titled "The Shame of the Schools."[13] Shattuck shows how the thick documents that purport to be "state standards" and "district curricula" are so generalized that they provide no real guidance to teachers. In one or two states, notably Massachusetts, the official guidelines have recently been made more specific (with consequent gains in achievement), but typically in the United States, state and district guidelines offer schools no definite information about grade-by-grade content. What sort of "local control" is that?

Let's look at one state's guidelines for language arts. (I won't reveal the state, since its request for me to review the document indicates its own dissatisfaction with them.) This state curriculum guide is quite typical. It is a 103-page document organized into a dozen broad categories, all of which apply to all the grades from kindergarten through grade twelve. The general categories have process rubrics like "Students shall demonstrate knowledge and understanding of media as a mode of communication," "Students shall employ a wide range of strategies as they write, using the writing process appropriately," and "Students shall apply a wide range of strategies to read and comprehend written materials." Then, in the more "detailed" amplifications of these categories for the early grades, we find directives like these: "Distinguish the purpose of various types of media presentations, using informational or entertainment presentations," "Use a variety of planning strategies/organizers," and "Draft information collected during reading and/or research into writing." For later grades the detailed amplifications are directives like "Write research reports that include a thesis and use a variety of sources" and "Read a variety of literature, including historical fiction, autobiography, and realistic fiction." The whole document is composed of similarly empty admonitions.

If calling these guidelines empty seems a harsh indictment, consider the following test to decide whether your own local standards actually determine a curriculum. Can you take another country's guidelines that really do define grade-by-grade content (say, the excellent Japanese or Finnish elementary guidelines) and, excluding the subject of local history, teach that curriculum and at the same time follow your local guidelines? Usually the answer is yes. As indicated, American guidelines are so vague that you can teach most of the Japanese or the Finnish curriculum and also follow the vague American guidelines without adding extra content. Let's consider the directive "Read a variety of literature, including historical fiction, autobiography, and realistic fiction." In the state guidelines I've been asked to evaluate, this rubric serves for grades five, six, and seven! Since not a single title is mentioned in the whole hundred-page document, it's not hard to see how this could be. Following this rubric for grades five, six, and seven, we could teach the Japanese language arts curriculum or the Finnish curriculum or the French curriculum or the Chinese curriculum (in translation, of course). American schools that wish to follow their own state standards as well as teach the detailed specifications of the Japanese curriculum (or, more appropriately, the grade-by-grade Core Knowledge Sequence) can readily do so without double duty.[14]

This illustrates the main shortcoming of these process-oriented, formalistic guidelines — they offer no real guidance. A second shortcoming is that such guidelines guarantee an incoherent education with huge gaps and boring repetitions. Elementary school students reasonably complain of reading *Charlotte's Web* three years in a row.

That's not too surprising. With guidelines like these, why should Mr. Green in grade three, Ms. Jones in grade four, and Ms. Hughes in grade five not treat their students to a book they are very fond of? Of course, while students are reading that estimable work three years running (being bored in two of them), they are missing at least two other estimable books they might have been introduced to.

This kind of problem is not limited to language arts. I once did an analysis of a district science curriculum which, like most American curricula, had a hands-on, formalistic, process orientation and found that students did a hands-on study of seeds in four different grades but were never required to learn about photosynthesis at all.[15] Gaps and repetitions are the reality of American students' school experience even when they stay in the same school, and the gaps are still greater for those many disadvantaged students who must change schools. These gaps and repetitions occur unwittingly, not through the fecklessness of guideline makers nor the incompetence of teachers but under the influence of very inadequate process theories. The resulting incoherence in the content to which the students are exposed is by itself enough to explain why, compared to students elsewhere, who experience a more coherent curriculum, American students fall further and further behind the longer they stay in school.

For students, the vagueness of the local guidelines produces an educational experience that is sparse, repetitious, incoherent, and fragmented. For teachers, the incoherence produces an intensely unsatisfactory professional experience, which induces a large percentage of them to leave the profession each year. One quarter of all beginning teachers quit their jobs within four years.[16] In urban settings, 50 percent of beginning teachers leave in five years or less.[17] They leave mainly because of low job satisfaction and stressful work conditions, not because they can make better salaries elsewhere.[18] Interestingly, one big cause of teacher dissatisfaction as well as student boredom seems to be the more chaotic character of the classroom at each successive grade level. American high school teachers are more dissatisfied with their jobs than elementary teachers, and fifth-grade teachers are more dissatisfied than first-grade teachers.[19]

One explanation for this gradual increase in teacher job dissatisfaction — the reason the teacher's task becomes more difficult and unpleasant with each grade level — may be that as American students advance through the grades, their preparation levels become ever more diverse. This was a finding that Stevenson and Stigler emphasized in *The Learning Gap*, a superb comparative study of American and Asian schools.[20] American teachers now take it as a matter of course that in the same classroom they must teach students who have gained and who have not gained the most basic knowledge they need to understand what is to be taught. Here we are speaking not about differences of ability but about huge differences in relevant preparation.

If the teacher directs the preponderance of instruction to students who haven't gained the prerequisite knowledge, the repetition of that basic knowledge to students who already know it is extremely boring. But if the teacher directs the class to those students who have gained the prerequisites, then the lagging students will fall still further behind. For both groups, the classroom will be boring. Boredom creates discipline problems, which further contribute to teachers' low job satisfaction. These are all effects that can be traced to the incoherence of the content that students experience under vague guidelines.

Stevenson and Stigler found that teachers have much greater job satisfaction when they can depend on one another in a supportive chain over the grade levels. Then all the students in a class can be counted on to have a reasonable level of preparation for the new grade level. This makes for a much happier situation for both the student and the teacher. In short, the doctrine that teachers have been instructed to hold — that their almost complete control over what they will teach is a plus for them — turns out, in considering the larger picture of curricular incoherence, to be a major cause of their professional unhappiness. By the same token, curricular incoherence is also the major cause of the inherent unfairness of our schooling. The unproductive use of school time, the changing content, the repetition, and the fragmentation that result from lack of specificity are bad for all students but are most disadvantageous to the already disadvantaged. The unparalleled vagueness of our curricular guides makes our system the most chaotic and unfair in the world.

THINKING THE UNTHINKABLE: A CORE OF COMMON CONTENT IN THE EARLY GRADES

By "commonality of content," I do not mean a 100 percent common curriculum across the nation under which each child in each early grade follows exactly the same course of study. I mean rather a more reasonable percentage of common content, such as Jefferson and Mann had in view — say, between 40 and 60 percent of the topics that young children are taught. But before I try to detach even that modest proposal from the realm of the unthinkable, I shall deal with a prior issue, a purely structural one — the grade level at which a widely-agreed-upon topic is introduced to children.

In the face of extensive student mobility, we need to reach agreement not only about what subject matter should be taught in school but also about the grade level at which that agreed-upon subject matter should be taught. Just as we have created a convention about the standard spelling of *Mississippi*, we need to create a convention about the grade level at which school topics shall be introduced. If we agree that primary-grade children should be taught about the *Mayflower*, then we have an obligation to decide when the *Mayflower* will be introduced. The ravages of mobility on disadvantaged students ought to exert a powerful moral claim in favor of such a policy, which deserves to trump local sentiments about whether kindergarten is or is not the right place for the *Mayflower*. No one can really answer that question in absolute terms. In most cases, questions about proper grade level have no absolute right answer, because, as Jerome Bruner famously observed, almost any topic, if taught appropriately, can be taught at any school age.[21]

But Bruner's insight emphatically does not argue for laissez-faire regarding the sequencing of topics. On the contrary, using an automotive analogy, either side of the road, appropriately demarcated, is suitable for driving in either direction — which is precisely why it is necessary to create a convention for determining whether the right side or the left side will be used. Whatever side of the road a state decides on, that same convention needs to hold for all roads in all the states, because cars cross state lines every day — just as disadvantaged students move every day across schools. The consequence of *not* creating a convention about the sequencing of agreed-upon topics is that some disadvantaged students will never hear about the *Mayflower* while others will hear about the *Mayflower* ad nauseam, in kindergarten, grade one, grade two, and beyond.

Mired in tradition, in anticontent ideas, and above all in complacency, we are one of the few nations to ignore the need for rationalizing a content sequence in the early grades. In the 1930s, struggling against his anticontent colleagues at Teachers College, the great William Bagley observed that we, of all nations, most need such commonality:

> The notion that each community must have a curriculum all its own is not only silly, but tragic. It neglects two important needs. The first, as we have already seen, is the need of a democracy for many common elements in the culture of all the people, to the end that the people may discuss collective problems in terms that will convey common meanings. The second need is extremely practical. It is the need of recognizing the fact that American people simply will not "stay put." They are the most mobile people in the world . . . Under these conditions, failure to have a goodly measure of uniformity in school subjects and grade placement is a gross injustice to at least ten million school children at the present time.[22]

As we have seen from the recent census reports, the injustice that Bagley identified in the 1930s now extends to many more than 10 million children. If we can reach consensus about a core of topics that should be taught, we are under a powerful moral and patriotic obligation to standardize the sequence and the grade level in which those topics are to be taught.

That's the first point. Let's call it the "When shall we teach the *Mayflower*?" question. But of course it is preceded by the "Shall we teach the *Mayflower* at all?" question, which is intellectually and politically the more difficult problem for liberal democracies. But it is a problem that we need to discuss openly. As I have shown in analyzing the "myth of the local curriculum," state and district guidelines typically do not mandate specific topics to be taught. I have also shown that this lack of specificity is equivalent in most areas of American schooling to having no mandated curriculum at all, much less a locally mandated one. It is true that some of the new state standards can point to increasingly specific guidance in a few areas, but these are the exception. In general, the de facto curriculum in the American school is whatever content is found in whatever textbooks are used and in selections made according to the tastes and beliefs of individual teachers. In other words, the curriculum in most American classrooms is an unknown curriculum. More openness about content specifics will reduce the liberal/conservative suspicions that are reasonably aroused by a hidden curriculum. One of the great advantages of discussing the hitherto untouchable topic of a nationwide sequence of core content is that an open, broad-daylight discussion of content is a protection against the hidden, secret, incoherent curriculum that has led to educational malfeasance, social unfairness, and cultural polarization.

For many years, my colleagues and I have wrestled with the "Shall we teach the *Mayflower* at all?" question. In 1987 I devoted a book to that issue. The combination of my scholarly specialties led me to realize that reading, writing, and all communication depend on hidden, taken-for-granted background knowledge that is not directly expressed in what is said or written. Therefore, in order to teach children how to understand what is said or written, we must teach them that taken-for-granted background knowledge. I hoped that this was a technical point on which all parties could agree, for we all want children to be able to read and communicate. It follows that we are obliged to give them the background knowledge they need to do so.

I was disappointed to discover that this simple (and scientifically correct) idea was opposed in the 1980s and 1990s not only by the powerful anticontent traditions of the education schools but also by many university intellectuals, who were not so sure we should teach the *Mayflower* and a lot of other traditional matter. Their aim was to improve and diversify American culture, not perpetuate it. This combination of forces — the anticontent ideas of the teaching profession and the let's-change-American-culture ideas of many intellectuals — has for several decades been delaying a descriptive approach to deciding what needs to be taught if children are to be able to read with comprehension. The ed school anticontent proponents are simply wrong. The culture-changing idealists, while often quite admirable, have oversimplified how the job of changing the culture can best be done, and have placed the burden of their ideals on the backs of disadvantaged children, who, because they are not gaining the traditional knowledge they need in order to read and write, are not learning to do so.

The tacit, taken-for-granted knowledge needed for general reading and writing in a speech community is by definition traditional knowledge. If it were untraditional, we could not be sure the other person knew it and we could not take it for granted. On the criterion of "What is assumed in speech?" we have an obligation to teach about the *Mayflower*. This technical principle for deciding what children need to know in order to join the literate speech community is, of course, just one principle for identifying the content we need to teach in the early grades. It does not include our ethical, civic, and aesthetic aspirations for education. But the technical principle is a big start. It is remarkable how much of the early curriculum in America can be built from this openly discussed technical principle, by simply asking the question, "Is this information often taken for granted in talk and writing addressed to a general literate audience?" As my colleagues at the Core Knowledge Foundation have shown, a very rich and interesting early education can be based on this principle. Striking examples of success from applying this approach can be found — disadvantaged students gaining ground, and all students gaining high literacy.

The states therefore need to agree with one another on a core of specifics. To do this, they will have to follow sounder principles than those that have produced current state standards. Current principles righteously proclaim their own virtue in being vague because they nurture the differences among children, leave freedom for the teacher and the district, and proclaim a commitment to "deeper" aims like critical thinking and understanding. These principles are unwitting masks for indecision and irresponsibility. Until they are removed, states can never reach decisions about the specific core content that the nation needs.

Currently, I know only a few persons in leadership positions who openly advocate that the states should agree on specific core content in all subjects in the early grades — Ruth Wattenberg, the brave editor of the *American Educator*, published by the American Federation of Teachers, and Diane Ravitch. More leaders should join them. In the face of high student mobility and the absolute need for literate background knowledge for enabling reading comprehension, those who present themselves as advocates of children and of the poor and the disadvantaged — all the many philanthropies and special educational organizations in the United States — should join forces and begin thinking the unthinkable about the early curriculum. Currently, these organizations support and encourage programs that are often effective at the level of the individual school. But by remaining at that level, they ignore the huge problem of mobility.

These organizations might lobby the states to cooperate in deciding on a grade-by-grade sequence of specific core topics in the early grades. They might mobilize their formidable intellectual and financial resources to show the public that commonality of curriculum topics does not mean mind control and that different schools can teach the same topics in various ways and still attain the degree of commonality we need to use school time productively and foster high literacy. These advocates of the disadvantaged should make the public aware that our precious independence and diversity are not submerged when we have a common base of allusion, any more than they are submerged when we have a common base of spelling and punctuation. Liberal and conservative philanthropies and child advocacy organizations should take the lead in pursuing this forbidden subject, so critical to our future. We also need a thoughtful liberal-conservative coalition that puts the general welfare above narrow sectarian interests — as Horace Mann hoped. At stake are fairness, solidarity, and the chance to live up to our ideals.

APPENDIX

NOTES

ACKNOWLEDGMENTS

INDEX

Appendix: The Critical Importance of an Adequate Theory of Reading

This appendix on the role of adequate scientific theory in reading and in education generally is included for those who wish to study more closely the research foundations and policy implications of this book. It attempts to explain why it is essential to go beyond the latest breathless reports from on-site studies, which are, even at their best, inconclusive. Good policy is made on the basis of theories that are most firmly grounded in the whole range of relevant empirical studies.

One of the most disdainful remarks in the hard sciences is that a piece of work is "atheoretical," meaning that it fails to relate the relevance of its factual findings to large complexes of phenomena and to more general scientific theories. Wolfgang Pauli once remarked about a scientific paper that "it is not even wrong."[1] Scientists regard the formulation of theories about deep causal factors to be the motive of scientific progress — a view that has rightly replaced an earlier just-the-facts conception of scientific advance.

What takes the place of scientific theory in much educational discourse is educational philosophy, which tends to be either liberal or conservative. As Private Willis explained in Act II of *Iolanthe*, "Every boy and every gal / That's born into the world alive / Is either a little liberal / Or else a little conservative." This partly explains the pattern of educational debates. Conservative "traditionalism" is often set against liberal "child-centered" education. Conservatives tend to think of human nature as something that needs to be molded. Liberals tend to think that the innate character of the child needs to be sympathetically nurtured and allowed to develop. Liberal and conservative theories of this sort are not lacking in American educational discourse. But that is not the kind of theory I mean in this appendix. Rather, I take the word in its scientific connotation, as a projection and generalization from what has been reliably learned in research.

Taking the word in that sense, there is too little theory in American education, especially with regard to ways of achieving agreed-upon goals, such as attaining proficiency in mathematics, reading, and writing. These goals themselves are not subjects of debate. Disagreements about how best to achieve them are, in principle, scientific debates. Yet there is a notable shortage of thoughtful scientific theory within educational discourse. That may be partly because educational research data tend to be uncertain. The uncontrolled variables in real classrooms — the social interactions of the class, the teacher's talents, the prior knowledge of the individual students — have made causal conclusions difficult to determine with confidence. Such difficulties were among the reasons given in a recent report of the National Research Council as to why no program or methods of teaching mathematics had been scientifically determined to be superior to any other.[2]

In reaction to such past defects of educational research, the Institute of Educational Sciences has recently instituted rigorous standards for data gathering, including an insistence on random assignments of students to experimental and control groups, on the pattern of good medical research. These are admirable advances. The more reliable the data we obtain are, the more reliable our theories will be. But good theory is not to be confused with good data-gathering techniques alone. The need for a deep general analysis is not obviated by even the best data-gathering techniques. The random assignment of students into control groups and experimental groups is an admirable method for gaining higher confidence in statistical results but cannot by itself explain the underlying reasons for the statistical results nor by itself allow confident predictions that they will be repeated in new circumstances.

Good data gathering does not by itself support the inference that what has worked in one place will work in another. It won't do to regard research results as a black box from which it can be directly argued, for instance, that since smaller class size led to better results in Tennessee, smaller classes will also lead to better results in California. The famous and expensive Tennessee STAR study (Student Achievement Teacher Ratio) was exemplary in its data-gathering techniques, using large numbers of students randomly assigned into control and experimental groups. Since the data gathering was so well conducted, policymakers in California reasoned that the results would apply to California and put that line of reasoning into effect at an estimated cost of $5 billion extra — without significant results. To infer reliably that carefully gathered results are replicable, one cannot treat them atheoretically. Data about what works in schools cannot necessarily simply be gathered from schools and then applied directly to improve different schools without the benefit of deep analysis and general predictive theory. To apply results elsewhere, one needs to understand in detail the causal factors that would allow confident predictions. What are the generalizable factors that make smaller class size more effective for earlier grades than for later ones? What are the replicable causes of student gain through smaller classes?

One important theoretical consideration too often neglected in educational research is that of opportunity cost. The multimillion-dollar Tennessee class-size study, while admirable for its random assignments and statistical punctiliousness, did not adequately address theoretical questions concerning unanalyzed opportunity costs. Could there be alternative, more reliable, and more cost-effective ways of achieving similar or higher gains? If, for example, an important advantage of smaller class size is more interaction time between student and teacher, are there alternative, less expensive policies for achieving more interaction time and still greater student gains? In other words, the Tennessee STAR study did not hazard a clear and detailed theoretical interpretation and generalization of its own findings. If it had, the state of California, basing its policy on the STAR study, might not have spent $5 billion in an unsuccessful effort to improve achievement simply through smaller class size.

Theory must always outrun data to provide a context for interpreting data and to justify predictions. Since educational data are often conflicted and uncertain, educational theories are too often simply ideological stances in disguise. It is against this backdrop that I proffer the following proposition: at any given time, it is our duty to work out the most probable theoretical analysis of a practical educational problem in the light of all the relevant research from all relevant areas, and to resist being distracted on the one side by the latest research bulletins and on the other side by people who say skeptically that educational data are too complex so we'll stick to our educational philosophy.

An adequate theory of reading will recognize that reading comprehension is a subcategory of language comprehension, and that language comprehension must entail attributes that often remain unmentioned in discussions of reading, especially the idea of the speech community. For communication to occur by means of language, the two sides (call them either speaker/listener or author/reader) have to learn and share the same language rules. For instance, a child learns that when a speaker says *you* to the child, it means the child, and when the speaker says *I*, it means the speaker. But when the child speaks, *I* means the child and *you* means the person being spoken to. The words take on different meanings — refer to different people — depending on the speaker, and this is a language rule that any comprehender must learn. A whole host of such tacit agreements are necessary to communication. The British philosopher H. P. Grice made a considerable reputation by explaining in a few pages the structure of many of these unspoken agreements.[3] The group of people who share these agreements is a speech community. Sharing the unsaid makes it possible for them to comprehend the said. It is the very thing that makes them a speech community.[4] Poor readers who can decode adequately but cannot comprehend well are usually readers who lack knowledge of a whole array of unspoken information being taken for granted by insiders in the speech community. To supply students with this unspoken, taken-for-granted knowledge as efficiently as possible should be the goal of a good reading program.

Scientific theories, explicit or implicit, have enormous practical ramifications. It was theory and not decisive data that caused current reading programs to include trivial, disconnected reading materials and to allot too much time and effort to the teaching of formal comprehension strategies. Proponents of the strategies could point to data that showed some improvements after a few weeks of strategy instruction. (Most educational interventions can supply positive data.) But these improvements were not large.[5] And long-term data regarding strategy instruction are even less impressive. If the long-term data favoring these practices had been decisive, we would not be having a nationwide reading comprehension problem. As I have suggested, the existing research on this issue better supports a contrary theory which is far more consistent with findings of cognitive science. This countertheory holds that extensive comprehension strategy instruction, while showing brief initial results for easily adduced reasons, is *not* a productive use of instructional time. This theory is well based on data and on a broad range of studies concerning the nature of language comprehension. Which theory is to be preferred?

A useful example of how to resolve conflict among empirical educational theories — until clearly decisive empirical results arrive

— comes from physics, a field in which there have been uncertainties just as great as those found in education. As recently as 1900 the existence of atoms was a matter of active dispute among scientists. The knotty theoretical problem of the existence of atoms goaded young Albert Einstein into his earliest work, from his doctoral dissertation of 1905 through several great articles on Avogadro's number (N) in 1905 and 1906. Einstein approached the question of N (the number of molecules in a given amount of matter) from a lot of different angles — blackbody radiation, the flow of solutions, Brownian motion, and the blue of the sky. He showed that all of these independent methods of determining N yielded a very similar number. Since each of these sources of computation was quite independent of the others, this independent convergence made it very hard to doubt the atomic theory. In framing theories that will guide fateful policy decisions about educating our children, this pattern of independent data convergence should be our goal.

In teaching children to become good readers, we need to ask hard questions about the relative efficiencies of conflicting instructional methods, several of which, like the STAR experiment, have an apparently good basis in research. The fact that a method has been shown to yield positive effects on reading comprehension or vocabulary gain doesn't mean that it meets the more stringent theoretical requirement of attaining these positive effects efficiently. These are the kinds of issues that a teacher, school administrator, or policymaker needs to have addressed, and it is the duty of the researcher who is familiar with both the data and the relevant literature to ponder and try to answer these theoretical questions about opportunity cost, quite apart from ideology and educational philosophy.

Coming back, then, to our example of strategy instruction, the theory supporting spending a lot of time in teaching reading comprehension strategies is a good example of nonconvergence. It is in conflict with much that has been learned about the gaining of expertise and the workings of the mind. The reading strategy theory initially took note of a narrow range of data: expert readers tend to monitor their own performances. Then the theory took an unwarranted leap: if that is what expert readers do, we will take a big shortcut by teaching novices how to monitor their performances. While some of the subsequent data did appear to support this approach, other data suggested that conscious self-monitoring is not the path that experts actually take to become experts. Studies of expertise have consistently shown a very slow development of high skill (ten years is close to the minimum time). Still other data indicate that active self-monitoring can be done effectively only after the person has become an expert — for reasons having to do with the limitations of channel capacity in the human mind. This evidence argues against burdening the novice's mind with self-conscious strategizing. Still another theoretical shortcoming of the strategy idea was its unspoken but incorrect assumption that these "metacognitive" comprehension strategies are formal, transferable activities that can be deployed independently of content knowledge. A better theory that accounted for a larger range of evidence would have avoided these scientific shortcomings and a tragic waste of classroom time.

Stressing the importance of theory might be considered a sign of indifference to educational data. But of course the contrary is the real case. Careful attention to achieving the most probable theory is the best way to take account of the greatest possible amount of relevant data. It's the best way of not being diverted from sound educational policy by some fresh bulletin from the schools that may or may not truly show what it claims to show. Suppose somebody comes up with a claim for a program that, according to research, can bring a child from low language comprehension to proficient language comprehension in one school year. This is not, perhaps, an absolute impossibility, but on strong theoretical grounds having to do with the gradual nature of knowledge and vocabulary acquisition, we need to be especially wary of claims to quick fixes in reading proficiency. There is a lot of evidence that although language development can be accelerated, it can never be really fast. We know this because we are beginning to have a deeper understanding of the way vocabulary and its accompanying knowledge is built up. This theoretical understanding can enable us to speed up progress in near-optimal fashion even as it repudiates the notion that Seabiscuit-style progress is possible in reading comprehension.

A theoretical understanding of the slow gradualism of gains in reading is an important consideration in taking practical steps toward implementing the practical recommendations of this book. Important test data on reading gains might not become available until a few years after these recommendations are put into practice. After three to five years, however, the gains predicted from theory (and from existing data) will be dramatic. Moreover, until a better theory of optimal reading instruction comes along, these reading gains should be considered the fastest gains that a school program can achieve. In general, as schooling proceeds on its slow, cumulative way, we continually need to rely on good theory — not on isolated pieces of data but rather on the largest possible array of data, which is what good theory by definition embraces.

The two ideologies or philosophies that dominate in the American educational world, which tend to corrupt scientific inferences, are naturalism and formalism. Naturalism is the notion that learning can and should be natural and that any unnatural or artificial approach to school learning should be rejected or deemphasized. This point of view favors many of the methods that are currently most praised and admired in early schooling — "hands-on learning," "developmentally appropriate practice," and the natural, whole-language method of learning to read. By contrast, methods that are unnatural are usually deplored, including "drill," "rote learning," and the analytical, phonics approach to teaching early reading. We call such naturalism an ideology rather than a theory because it is more a value system (based historically on the European Romantic movement) than an empirically based idea. If we adopt this ideology, we know in advance that the natural is good and the artificial is bad. We don't need analysis and evidence; we are certain, quite apart from evidence, that children's education will be more productive if it is more natural. If the data do not show this, it is because we are using the wrong kinds of data, such as scores on standardized tests. That is naturalism.

Formalism is the ideology that what counts in education is not the learning of things but rather learning how to learn. What counts is not gaining mere facts but gaining formal skills. Along with naturalism, it shares an antipathy to mere facts and to the piling up of information. The facts, it says, are always changing. Children need to learn how to understand and interpret any new facts that come along. The skills that children need to learn in school are not how to follow mindless procedures but rather how to understand what lies behind the procedures so they can apply them to new situations. In reading, instead of learning a lot of factual subject matter, which is potentially infinite, the child needs to learn strategies for dealing with any texts, such as "questioning the author," "classifying," and other "critical thinking" skills.

Both naturalism and formalism are powerful because they are attractive and, rightly understood, contain much truth. We would all be better off if they were entirely true, in which case American schools would be making a far better showing on international comparisons. But insofar as they function as empirical theories, they are in their unqualified forms very inadequate and are at odds with what is known in relevant scientific fields.

Naturalism is at least partly wrong in all those cases where the things to be learned (like alphabetic decoding) are historically late, artificial products of civilization. There is no natural, innate alphabetic learning faculty in children's minds comparable to their innate oral language faculty. Naturalism is mainly right about first-language learning and, as we observed in Chapter 4, about vocabulary acquisition, but it is in error in trying to conflate oral language learning and alphabetic phonics. Similarly, the base-ten number system, like the alphabet, is a nonnatural system, and there are no good empirical grounds for thinking that a naturalistic approach to learning the operations of the base-ten system will work very well, as in fact it does not. However, it is also very unlikely that a harsh, unnatural, drill-and-kill approach to either the alphabet or the base-ten system will work best with young children. Consideration of the defects and strengths of naturalism, embracing what psychology knows about these issues, is best described not as part of a fight-to-the-death, liberal-vs.-conservative ideology but simply as a sounder empirical theory.

The same qualifications need to be made about the ideology of formalism. In some respects the learning-to-learn idea is correct. It is true, for example, that the child needs to be able to learn new things through reading. It would therefore appear necessary that learning how to learn is a more important educational goal than learning mere facts and subject matter. But we have already alluded to the firm empirical finding that in order to understand a text, the child has to have prior knowledge about its domain. That would argue for the theory that teaching the child a lot of domains is itself a necessary element in learning to learn. This suggests a theoretical middle ground between formalism and antiformalism. The antiformalists are right to stress that general reading ability must necessarily be founded upon general knowledge — on a lot of "mere information." The formalists are right to insist that the goal of such an education is not primarily to possess this information in itself but to possess it as a means of learning to learn. Externally, therefore, the formalist goal is one that can be accepted. What good empirical theory has to offer is the complicating insight that the only way to achieve the goal of learning to learn is through something that the formalist ideologue disdains — a lot of diverse information.

In short, a new watchword in education needs to be not only "random assignment" but also "convergence," which is a criterion that will require a lot of scientific knowledge and thought.[6] The young Einstein gave a memorable explanation of the principle of convergence from multiple domains when he was still a patent clerk. He received a report from an eminent experimenter that was inconsistent with his theory that the mass of an electron increases with its velocity by a certain amount. The experimenter's work had been done very carefully, and Einstein's friend and mentor H. A. Lorentz was ready to give up the theory in view of the unfavorable data. But young Einstein was aware that experimental setups are subject to uncontrolled variables, and in a published review of the subject had this to say in 1907:

> It will be possible to decide whether the foundations of the theory correspond with the facts only if a great variety of observations is at hand . . . In my opinion, both [the alternative theories of Abraham and Bucherer] have rather slight probability, because their fundamental assumptions concerning the mass of moving electrons are not explainable in terms of theoretical systems which embrace a greater complex of phenomena.[7]

The key phrases are "great variety of observations" and "embrace a greater complex of phenomena." Ultimately Einstein was shown to be correct, and the overhasty inferences from rigorous but narrow data gathering were wrong. Einstein understood the critical importance of accepting for the time being only those conceptions that converge independently from the widest complexes of phenomena.

This is a point that Steven Weinberg makes very amusingly. Using the example of medical research, which is similar to educational research in many respects, he cautions that mere experimental and statistical methods can be highly dubious without the explanatory support of fundamental science.

> Medical research deals with problems that are so urgent and difficult that proposals of new cures often must be based on medical statistics without understanding how the cure works, but even if a new cure were suggested by experience with many pa-

tients, it would probably be met with skepticism if one could not see how it could possibly be explained reductively, in terms of sciences like biochemistry and cell biology. Suppose that a medical journal carried two articles reporting two different cures for scrofula: one by ingestion of chicken soup and the other by a king's touch. Even if the statistical evidence presented for these two cures had equal weight, I think the medical community (and everyone else) would have very different reactions to the two articles. Regarding chicken soup I think that most people would keep an open mind, reserving judgment until the cure could be confirmed by independent tests. Chicken soup is a complicated mixture of good things, and who knows what effect its contents might have on the mycobacteria that cause scrofula? On the other hand, whatever statistical evidence were offered to show that a king's touch helps to cure scrofula, readers would tend to be very skeptical because they would see no way that such a cure could ever be explained reductively . . . How could it matter to a mycobacterium whether the person touching its host was properly crowned and anointed or the eldest son of the previous monarch?[8]

Without greater theoretical sophistication, we are unlikely to achieve better practical results in education. With greater theoretical sophistication, educational research might begin to earn the prestige that it currently lacks but, given its potential importance, could some day justify. The place to begin is with reading.

Notes

1. WHY DO WE HAVE A KNOWLEDGE DEFICIT?

1. International Association for the Evaluation of Educational Achievement, *Progress in International Reading Literacy Study* (PIRLS) (Chestnut Hill, Mass.: PIRLS International Study Center, 2001); *Program for International Student Assessment* (PISA), Measuring Student Knowledge and Skills (Paris: Organization for Economic Cooperation and Development, 2000); Mariann Lemke . . . [et al.]; National Center for Education Statistics Educational Resources Information, *Outcomes of learning results from the 2000 Program for International Student Assessment of 15-year-olds in reading, mathematics, and science literacy* (Washington, D.C.: U.S. Dept. of Education, 2001; Laurence T. Ogle et al., *International comparisons in fourth-grade reading literacy: Findings from the Progress in International Reading Literacy Study (PIRLS) of 2001* (Washington, D.C.: National Center for Education Statistics, 2003).

2. Anne E. Cunningham and Keith E. Stanovich, "Early Reading Acquisition and Its Relation to Reading Experience and Ability 10 Years Later," *Developmental Psychology* 33, 6 (Nov. 1997): 934–45.

3. William R. Johnson and Derek Neal, "Basic Skills and the Black-White Earnings Gap," in Christopher Jencks and Meredith Phillips, eds., *The Black-White Test Score Gap* (Washington, D.C.: Brookings Institution, 1998), pp. 480–97.

4. National Center for Education Statistics Educational Resources Information, *National Assessment of Educational Progress (NAEP), Reading*

Assessments (Washington, D.C.: U.S. Dept. of Education, 1998 and 2002). I've just received the welcome news of an improvement by nine-year-olds, both in overall reading proficiency and in narrowing the gap between groups, but there has been no improvement in the later grades, when reading comprehension rather than decoding becomes the more important element. This is the usual pattern. Needless to say, the real result of our education — how well our middle school and high school graduates comprehend what they read — is the critical test of our schooling. See http://nces.ed.gov/nationsreportcard/ltt/results2004/ and Nick Anderson, "Schools Shift Approach as Adolescent Readers Fail to Improve," *Washington Post*, Aug. 1, 2005, p. B1.

5. E. D. Hirsch, *The Schools We Need and Why We Don't Have Them* (New York: Doubleday, 1996), p. 43.

6. Vernon Louis Parrington, *Main Currents in American Thought: An Interpretation of American Literature from the Beginnings to 1920* (New York: Harcourt, Brace, 1927–31).

7. "Natural men's prudence and care to preserve their own lives, or the care of others to preserve them, do not secure them a moment." Jonathan Edwards, 1741.

8. Horace Mann, *Seventh Annual Report, 1843*, in *Report Together with the Report of the Secretary of the Board, 1st–12th* (Boston: Dalton, 1838–1849).

9. That is not to say that the word *development* has no proper place at all in our thinking about education. In the very early years, when the brain is still maturing physiologically, there is a nearly universal sequence of learning. Perhaps the best recent book about the appropriate limits of the development idea in early childhood learning is Robert Siegler, *Emerging Minds: The Process of Change in Children's Thinking* (New York: Oxford University Press, 1998). See also R. Siegler and M. W. Alibali, *Children's Thinking* (New York: Prentice-Hall, 2005).

10. For the half that is true, see Siegler, *Emerging Minds*, and Siegler and Alibali, *Children's Thinking*.

11. Eric T. Bell, *The Development of Mathematics* (New York: McGraw-Hill, 1940) and David M. Burton, *The History of Mathematics: An Introduction* (Boston: Allyn & Bacon, 1985).

12. John Noble Wilford, "Who Began Writing? Many Theories, Few Answers," *New York Times*, Apr. 6, 1999, and David Sacks, *Letter Perfect:*

The Marvelous History of Our Alphabet from A to Z (New York: Broadway, 2004).

13. Richard Hofstadter, *Anti-Intellectualism in American Life* (New York: Vintage Books, 1963).

14. Adrienne Koch and William Peden, eds., *The Life and Selected Writings of Thomas Jefferson* (New York: Modern Library, 1944).

15. "Next to make them expert in the usefullest points of Grammar, and withall to season them, and win them early to the love of vertue and true labour, ere any flattering seducement, or vain principle seise them wandering, some easie and delightful Book of Education would be read to them; whereof the Greeks have store, as *Cebes, Plutarch,* and other Socratic discourses. But in Latin we have none of classic authority extant, except the two or three first Books of *Quintilian,* and some select pieces elsewhere. But here the main skill and groundwork will be, to temper them such Lectures and Explanations upon every opportunity, as may lead and draw them in willing obedience, enflam'd with the study of Learning, and the admiration of Vertue; . . . At the same time, some other hour of the day, might be taught them the rules of Arithmetick, and soon after the Elements of Geometry even playing, as the old manner was. After evening repast, till bed-time their thoughts will be best taken up in the easie grounds of Religion, and the story of Scripture. The next step would be to the Authors of *Agriculture, Cato, Varro,* and *Columella,* for the matter is most easie, and if the language be difficult, so much the better, it is not a difficulty above their years." John Milton, "Of Education" 1644.

16. Emerson *Journals,* entry for September 14, 1839, in *The Heart of Emerson's Journals,* eds. Bliss and Perry (Boston: Houghton Mifflin, 1937).

17. Jeanne S. Chall, Vicki A. Jacobs, Luke E. Baldwin, *The Reading Crisis: Why Poor Children Fall Behind* (Cambridge, Mass.: Harvard University Press, 1990).

18. Cunningham and Stanovich, *Early Reading Acquisition.*

19. Here is a characteristic summary from a present-day inheritor of these ideas: "Critical thinking is the use of those cognitive skills or strategies that increase the probability of a desirable outcome. It is used to describe thinking that is purposeful, reasoned and goal directed — the kind of thinking involved in solving problems, formulating inferences, calculating likelihoods, and making decisions when the thinker is using skills that are thoughtful and effective for the particular context

and type of thinking task. Critical thinking also involves evaluating the thinking process — the reasoning that went into the conclusion we've arrived at the kinds of factors considered in making a decision. Critical thinking is sometimes called directed thinking because it focuses on a desired outcome." Diane F. Halpern, *Thought and Knowledge: An Introduction to Critical Thinking* (Mahwah, N.J.: Erlbaum, 1996).

20. For reviews of the scientific literature on these subjects, see E. D. Hirsch, *Cultural Literacy* (Boston: Houghton Mifflin, 1987), Hirsch, *The Schools We Need*, W. Schneider, J. Korkel, and F. E. Weinert, "Expert Knowledge, General Abilities, and Text Processing," in W. Schneider and F. E. Weinert, eds., *Interactions Among Aptitudes, Strategies, and Knowledge in Cognitive Performance* (New York: Springer-Verlag, 1990).

21. Linda Perlstein, "School Pushes Reading, Writing Reform; Sciences Shelved to Boost Students to 'No Child' Standard," *Washington Post*, May 31, 2004, p. A1.

22. Max Planck, *Scientific Autobiography and Other Papers*, Frank Gaynor, trans. (London: Williams & Norgate, 1950): "A new scientific truth does not triumph by convincing its opponents and making them see the light, but rather because its opponents eventually die and a new generation grows up that is familiar with it."

23. Hideki Hiroishi, Akio Iwasaki, and Masahiko Oe, *Comparative Study of Cross-Cultural Understanding: Japan and the United States: Cultural Traits and Curriculum as Crucial Agents*, http://www.cck.dendai.ac.jp/~hiroishi/Report/eno1.html: "We found a significant difference in the length of time students spend watching television. While the most American students watch TV 'one–two hours a day,' their Japanese counterparts responded that they watch TV 'more than three hours a day.' This tendency is more conspicuous among high schoolers. Whereas three quarters of Japanese high school students spend more than two hours a day watching TV, the largest high school viewing population was found among those students who watch TV thirty minutes to an hour a day in the U.S."

24. Richard Rothstein, *Class and Schools: Using Social, Economic, and Educational Reform to Close the Black-White Achievement Gap* (Washington, D.C.: Economic Policy Institute, c2004).

25. Among the many research reports on this subject, the following are

notable: A. Garnham and J. Oakhill, "The Mental Models Theory of Language Comprehension," in B. K. Britton and A. C. Graesser, eds., *Models of Understanding Text* (Hillsdale, N.J.: Erlbaum, 1996); Arthur C. Graesser and Rolf A. Zwaan, "Inference Generation and the Construction of Situation Models," in Charles A. Weaver III, Suzanne Mannes, and Charles R. Fletcher, eds., *Discourse Comprehension: Essays in Honor of Walter Kintsch* (Hillsdale, N.J.: Erlbaum, 1995), pp. 117–39; Walter Kintsch, *Comprehension: A Paradigm for Cognition* (New York: Cambridge University Press, 1998); H. van Oostendorp and S. R. Goldman, eds., *The Construction of Mental Representations During Reading* (Mahwah, N.J.: Erlbaum, 1999); Rolf A. Zwaan, and Gabriel A. Radvansky, "Situation Models in Language Comprehension and Memory," *Psychological Bulletin* 123, 2 (Mar. 1998): 162–85.

26. Geraldine J. Clifford and James W. Guthrie, *Ed School: A Brief for Professional Education* (Chicago: University of Chicago Press, 1988); Diane Ravitch, *Left Back: A Century of Failed School Reforms* (New York: Simon & Schuster, 2000); Hirsch, *The Schools We Need*.

2. SOUNDING OUT: JUST THE BEGINNING OF READING

1. Marilyn Jager Adams, *Beginning to Read: Thinking and Learning About Print* (Cambridge, Mass.: MIT Press, 1990); Jeanne Chall, *Learning to Read: The Great Debate* (New York: McGraw-Hill, 1967).

2. This evidence is summarized in National Institute of Child Health and Human Development, *Report of the National Reading Panel: Teaching Children to Read* (Washington, D.C.: National Institutes of Health, 2000).

3. "Marion Joseph Steps Down," *Education Week* Jan. 29, 2003, p. 16.

4. See, for example, Steven A. Stahl, *Vocabulary Development* (Cambridge, Mass.: Brookline, 1999).

5. Stephanie Caillies, Guy Denhiere, and Walter Kintsch, "The Effect of Prior Knowledge on Understanding from Text: Evidence from Primed Recognition," *European Journal of Cognitive Psychology* 14, 2 (Apr. 2002): 267–86.

6. Keith E. Stanovich, "Matthew Effects in Reading: Some Consequences of Individual Differences in the Acquisition of Literacy," *Reading Research Quarterly* 21, 4 (Fall 1986):360–407.

7. Betty Hart, and Todd R. Risley, *Meaningful Differences in the Every-day Experience of Young American Children* (Baltimore: Peter Brookes, 1995).

8. Kate Walsh, "Basal Readers: The Lost Opportunity to Build the Knowledge that Propels Comprehension," *American Educator* 27, 1 (Spring 2003): 24–27.

9. Alan D. Baddeley, *Human Memory: Theory and Practice* (Needham Heights, Mass.: Allyn & Bacon, 1998).

10. Thomas G. Sticht et al., *Auding and Reading: A Developmental Model* (Alexandria, Va: Human Resources Research Organization, July 1974), U.S. AFHRL Technical Report. No. 74–36, 116.

11. This may not be so in cases of severe dyslexia, of course. See S. Shay-witz, *Overcoming Dyslexia: A New and Complete Science-Based Program for Reading Problems at Any Level* (New York: Knopf, 2004).

12. E. D. Hirsch, *Cultural Literacy* (Boston: Houghton Mifflin, 1987).

13. From *Morning Edition*, July 5, 2004, National Public Radio. Quoted with permission.

14. Meeting in the Oval Office, Mar. 23, 1971, from transcripts held at U.S. Archives, available at http://www.archives.gov/nixon/tapes/transcripts/connally_exhibit_1.pdf.

15. E. D. Hirsch, Jr., *The Philosophy of Composition* (Chicago: University of Chicago Press, 1977), pp. 51–72.

16. T. M. Griffin, L. Hemphill, L. Camp, and D. P. Wolf, "Oral Discourse in the Preschool Years and Later Literacy Skills," *First Language* 24, 2 (June 2004): 123–47.

17. C. Juel, "Learning to Read and Write: A Longitudinal Study of 54 Children from First to Fourth Grade," *Journal of Educational Psychology* 80, 4 (1988): 437–47. See also D. J. Francis, S. E. Shaywitz, K. K. Steubing, B. A. Shaywitz, and J. M. Fletcher, "Developmental Lag Versus Deficit Models of Reading Disability: A Longitudinal Individual Growth Curves Analysis," *Journal of Educational Psychology* 88, 1 (1996): 3–17.

18. Donna R. Recht and Lauren Leslie, "Effect of Prior Knowledge on Good and Poor Readers' Memory of Text," *Journal of Educational Psychology* 80, 1 (Mar. 1988): 16–20.

19. W. Schneider and J. Korkel, "The Knowledge Base and Text Recall: Evidence from a Short-Term Longitudinal Study," *Contemporary Educational Psychology* 14 (1989): 382–93: "Performance was more a function of soccer knowledge than of aptitude level."

20. M. Singer, R. Revlin, and M. Halldorson, "Bridging-Inferences and Enthymemes," in A. C. Graesser and G. H. Bower, eds., *Inferences and Text Comprehension* (San Diego: Academic, 1990), pp. 35–52.

21. Arthur C. Graesser, Murray Singer, and Tom Trabasso, "Constructing Inferences During Narrative Text Comprehension," *Psychological Review* 101, 3 (July 1994): 371–95, and Arthur C. Graesser and Rolf A. Zwaan, "Inference Generation and the Construction of Situation Models," in Charles A. Weaver III, Suzanne Mannes, et al., eds., *Discourse Comprehension: Essays in Honor of Walter Kintsch* (Hillsdale, N.J.: Erlbaum, 1995), pp. 117–39.

22. There is a large literature on the decline of verbal SAT scores in the 1960s and 1970s, and on NAEP (National Assessment of Educational Progress) scores when these began to be collected in the 1970s. The self-gratulatory claim that these large declines can be attributed to a broader test-taking population (that is, Hispanics and blacks did not take them before) is refuted by the significant decline in the absolute numbers of students scoring in the top categories. The increase in minority test-takers did not induce a decline in the absolute numbers of white test-takers; hence, an absolute decline in the number of high scorers could not have been caused by democratization of the test-taking population. A summary of these issues with full bibliographical references can be found in Hirsch, *Cultural Literacy*, pp. 1–10, and *The Schools We Need*, pp. 39–42, 176–79.

23. The best discussion of this issue is still that of Christopher Jencks: "What's Behind the Drop in Test Scores?" *Working Papers*. Department of Sociology, Harvard University, Cambridge, Mass., July–Aug. 1978.

24. www.bankstreet.edu/literacy guide/back.html, July 15, 2004.

25. W. Kintsch, "The Role of Knowledge in Discourse Comprehension: A Construction Integration Model," *Psychological Review* 95 (1988): 163–82; P. Karen Murphy and Patricia A. Alexander, "What Counts? The Predictive Powers of Subject-Matter Knowledge, Strategic Processing, and Interest in Domain-Specific Performance," *Journal of Experimental Education* 70, 3 (Spring 2002): 197–214; Rolf A. Zwaan and Gabriel A. Radvansky, "Situation Models in Language Comprehension and Memory," *Psychological Bulletin* 123, 2 (Mar. 1998): 162–85.

26. The earliest technical use of the term "situation model" that I have found is in Teun A. van Dijk and Walter Kintsch, *Strategies of Discourse Comprehension* (New York: Academic, 1983).

27. *Mcculloch* v. *Maryland*, 1819.

28. Robert M. Krauss and Sam Glucksberg, "Social and Nonsocial Speech," *Scientific American* 236, 2 (Feb. 1977): 100–105; Andrew Radford, Martin Atkinson, David Britain, Harald Clahsen, and Andrew Spencer, *Linguistics: An Introduction* (New York: Cambridge University Press, 1999).

29. Walsh, "Basal Readers."

30. Scott Foresman Reading, Grade One, Volume 6, *Surprise Me* (Glenview, Ill.: Addison-Wesley, 2000).

31. See Malcolm Gladwell, "The Art Of Failure," *The New Yorker,* Aug. 2000: "These two learning systems are quite separate, based in different parts of the brain. Willingham says that when you are first taught something — say, how to hit a backhand or an overhead forehand — you think it through in a very deliberate, mechanical manner. But as you get better the implicit system takes over: you start to hit a backhand fluidly, without thinking . . . Under conditions of stress, however, the explicit system sometimes takes over. That's what it means to choke. When Jana Novotna faltered at Wimbledon, it was because she began thinking about her shots again. She lost her fluidity, her touch. She double-faulted on her serves and mis-hit her overheads, the shots that demand the greatest sensitivity in force and timing. She seemed like a different person — playing with the slow, cautious deliberation of a beginner — because, in a sense, she was a beginner again: she was relying on a learning system that she hadn't used to hit serves and overhead forehands and volleys since she was first taught tennis, as a child."

32. Barak Rosenshine and Carla Meister, "Reciprocal Teaching: A Review of the Research," *Review of Educational Research* 64, 4 (Winter 1994) 479–530.

33. M. Pressley, "What Should Comprehension Instruction Be the Instruction of?" In Michael L. Kamil, Peter B. Mosenthal, David Pearson, and Rebecca Barr, eds., *Handbook of Reading Research,* Vol. 3 (Mahwah, N.J.: Erlbaum, 2000).

34. Rosenshine and Meister, "Reciprocal Teaching."

35. T. Trabasso and S. Suh, "Understanding Text: Achieving Explanatory Coherence Through On-line Inferences and Mental Operations in Working Memory," *Discourse Processes* 16 (1993): 3–34.

36. Shelly Dews et al., "Children's Understanding of the Meaning and Functions of Verbal Irony," *Child Development* 67, 6 (Dec. 1996): 3071–

85; Kina D. Leitner, "Children's Recognition of Double Meanings," *Dissertation Abstracts International* 53, 3-B (Sept. 1992): 1623.

3. KNOWLEDGE OF LANGUAGE

1. See, for example, W. F. Leopold, "The Decline of German Dialects," in J. A. Fishman, ed., *Readings in the Sociology of Language* (The Hague, 1968).

2. O. Jespersen, *Progress in Language with Special Reference to English* (London, 1894); *Language, Its Nature, Development, and Origin* (London, 1922); *Efficiency in Language Change* (Copenhagen, 1941).

3. Some versions of Black American English contain both the standard forms and the *be* forms, and the *be* forms can be described as habitual aspect markers that do not exist in Standard American English.

4. M. M. Guxman, "Some General Regularities in the Formation and Development of National Languages," in Fishman, ed., *Readings in the Sociology of Language*, pp. 773–76.

5. These date back to a position statement put out by the National Council of Teachers of English called "Students' Right to Their Own Language," *College Composition and Communication* 25 (Fall 1974). This statement was reaffirmed by the NCTE in 2003. See http://www.ncte.org/about/over/positions/category/div/114918.htm.

> The resolution is as follows:
>
> Resolved, that the National Council of Teachers of English affirm the students' right to their own language — to the dialect that expresses their family and community identity, the idiolect that expresses their unique personal identity; that NCTE affirm the responsibility of all teachers of English to assist all students in the development of their ability to speak and write better whatever their dialects; that NCTE affirm the responsibility of all teachers to provide opportunities for clear and cogent expression of ideas in writing, and to provide the opportunity for students to learn the conventions of what has been called written edited American English; and that NCTE affirm strongly that teachers must have the experiences and training that will enable them to understand and respect diversity of dialects. Be it further Resolved, that, to this end, the NCTE make available to other professional organizations this resolution as well as suggestions for ways of dealing with linguistic variety, as expressed in the CCCC background statement on students' right to their own lan-

guage; and that NCTE promote classroom practices to expose students
to the variety of dialects that comprise our multiregional, multiethnic,
and multicultural society, so that they too will understand the nature of
American English and come to respect all its dialects.

6. For a discussion of these early controversies that have persisted, see
    E. D. Hirsch, Jr., "The Normative Character of Written Speech," in
    The Philosophy of Composition (Chicago: University of Chicago Press,
    1977).

7. W. Wolfram, C. T. Adger, and Donna Christian, *Dialects in Schools and
    Communities* (Mahwah, N.J.: Erlbaum, 1999).

8. See, for instance, Hanni U. Taylor, *Standard English, Black English, and
    Bidialectalism: A Controversy* (New York: Peter Lang, 1989).

9. B. Bernstein, "Social Class, Language, and Socialization," in P. P.
    Giglioli, ed., *Language and Social Context* (Harmondsworth, England:
    Penguin, 1972).

10. Betty Hart and Todd R. Risley, *Meaningful Differences in the Every-
    day Experience of Young American Children* (Baltimore: Peter Brookes,
    1995).

11. W. Labov, "The Logic of Nonstandard English," in Giglioli, *Language
    and Social Context.*

12. Bernstein, "Social Class, Language, and Socialization," pp. 167–68.

13. Charles Darwin, *The Formation of Vegetable Mould Through the Action
    of Worms with Observations on Their Habits* (Ontario, Calif.: Book-
    worm, 1976).

14. Steven Pinker, *Words and Rules: The Ingredients of Language* (New
    York: Basic, 1999).

15. Joan P. Gipe and Richard D. Arnold, "Teaching Vocabulary Through
    Familiar Associations and Contexts," *Journal of Reading Behavior* 11, 3
    (Fall 1979); 281–85; Diana Christine Pulido, "The Impact of Topic Fa-
    miliarity, L2 Reading Proficiency, and L2 Passage Sight Vocabulary on
    Incidental Vocabulary Gain Through Reading for Adult Learners of
    Spanish as a Foreign Language," *Dissertation Abstracts International,*
    Vol. 61(10-A), May 2001, 3892.

16. Thomas K. Landauer and Susan T. Dumais, "A Solution to Plato's
    Problem: The Latent Semantic Analysis Theory of Acquisition, Induc-
    tion, and Representation of Knowledge," *Psychological Review* 104, 2
    (Apr. 1997): 211–40.

17. I. S. P. Nation, *Teaching and Learning Vocabulary* (New York: Newbury

House, 1990); S. A. Stahl, *Vocabulary Development* (Cambridge, Mass.: Brookline Books, 1999).

18. Anne E. Cunningham and Keith E. Stanovich, "Early Reading Acquisition and Its Relation to Reading Experience and Ability 10 Years Later," *Developmental Psychology* 33, 6 (Nov. 1997): 934–45.

19. Anne E. Cunningham and Keith E. Stanovich, "What Reading Does for the Mind," *American Educator* (Spring/Summer 1998): 2–3; D. P. Hayes and M. Ahrens, "Speaking and Writing: Distinct Patterns of Word Choice," *Journal of Memory and Language* 27 (1988): 572–85; Chafe and Danielewicz, "Properties of Spoken and Written Language," in Horowitz and Samuels, eds., *Comprehending Oral and Written Language* (San Diego: Academic, 1987), pp. 83–113.

20. Andrew Biemiller and Naomi Slonim, "Estimating Root Word Vocabulary Growth in Normative and Advantaged Populations: Evidence for a Common Sequence of Vocabulary Acquisition," *Journal of Educational Psychology* 93, 3 (Sept. 2001): 498–520; Andrew Biemiller, "Vocabulary: Needed If More Children Are to Read Well," *Reading Psychology* 24, 3-4 (July-Sept. 2003): 323–35; Isabel L. Beck, Margaret G. McKeown, and Richard C. Omanson, "The Effects and Uses of Diverse Vocabulary Instructional Techniques," in Margaret G. McKeown and Mary E. Curtis, eds., *The Nature of Vocabulary Acquisition* (Hillsdale, N.J.: Erlbaum, 1987), pp. 147–63; Richard C. Omanson, Isabel L. Beck, Margaret G. McKeown, and Charles A. Perfetti, "Comprehension of Texts with Unfamiliar Versus Recently Taught Words: Assessment of Alternative Models," *Journal of Educational Psychology* 76, 6 (Dec. 1984): 1253–68; Richard C. Anderson and William E. Nagy, "Word Meanings," in Rebecca Barr et al., eds., *Handbook of Reading Research*, Vol. 2 (Hillsdale, N.J.: Erlbaum, 1991) pp. 690–724; William E. Nagy, Richard C. Anderson, and Patricia A. Herman, "Learning Word Meanings from Context During Normal Reading," *American Educational Research Journal* 24, 2 (Summer 1987): 237–70. George A. Miller, "On Knowing a Word," *Annual Review of Psychology* 50 (1999): 1–19; Thomas K. Landauer and Susan T. Dumais, "A Solution to Plato's Problem: The Latent Semantic Analysis Theory of Acquisition, Induction, and Representation of Knowledge," *Psychological Review* 104, 2 (Apr. 1997): 211–40.

21. For a contrary view, see A. Biemiller and N. Slomin, "Estimating Root Word Vocabulary Growth in Normative and Advantaged Populations:

Evidence for a Common Sequence of Vocabulary Acquisition," *Journal of Educational Psychology* 93 (2001): 498–520; E. B. Zechmeister, A. M. Chronis, et al., "Growth of a Functionally Important Lexicon," *Journal of Reading Behavior* 27 (1995): 201–12.

22. Isabel L. Beck, Margaret G. McKeown, and Linda Kucan, *Bringing Words to Life: Robust Vocabulary Instruction* (New York: Guilford, 2002).

23. Ferdinand de Saussure, *Course in General Linguistics*, Charles Bally and Albert Sechehaye, eds., Roy Harris, trans. (London: Duckworth, 1983).

24. Steven Pinker, *The Language Instinct* (New York: Morrow, 1994).

25. National Reading Panel, *Report of the National Reading Panel: Teaching Children to Read* (Washington, D.C.: National Institute of Child Health and Human Development, National Institutes of Health, 2000).

26. To be precise, the naturalists are wrong to assume that a big vocabulary develops naturally through contact with everyday spoken language. A basic vocabulary does develop that way, but in order to insure that all children develop a rich vocabulary adequate for reading comprehension, we need to create artificial contexts — contexts in which children are exposed to print, first by listening to reading and later by reading on their own. The natural word-learning mechanism only works well if exposure to new words is carefully contextualized through parent or teacher artifice.

27. Landauer and Dumais, "A Solution to Plato's Problem."

28. Miller, "On Knowing a Word."

29. Nagy, Anderson, and Herman, "Learning Word Meanings from Context During Normal Reading."

30. Hayes and Ahrens, "Speaking and Writing: Distinct Patterns of Word Choice"; Cunningham and Stanovich, "What Reading Does for the Mind," pp. 2–3; Keith E. Stanovich, "Does Reading Make You Smarter? Literacy and the Development of Verbal Intelligence," in Hayne W. Reese, ed., *Advances in Child Development and Behavior*, Vol. 24 (San Diego: Academic, 1993) pp. xii, 317.

31. Stanovich, "Does Reading Make You Smarter?"

32. See M. Duthoit, "L'enfant et l'école: Aspects synthetiques du suivi d'un echantillon de vingt mille élèves des écoles, *Education et Formations* 16 (1988): 3–13. Some of the relevant French research has been translated and can be found at http://www.coreknowledge.org/CKproto2/Preschool/FrenchEquity.htm.

4. KNOWLEDGE OF THINGS

1. Carlo M. Cipolla, *Literacy and Development in the West* (Harmondsworth, Eng.: Penguin, 1969); E. D. Hirsch, *The Philosophy of Composition* (Chicago: Chicago University Press, 1977).

2. Teun A. van Dijk and Walter Kintsch, *Strategies of Discourse Comprehension* (New York: Academic, 1983).

3. Bengt Altenberg and Sylviane Granger, eds., *Lexis in Contrast: Corpus-Based Approaches* (Amsterdam: John Benjamins, 2002); R. Piotrowski, "Psycholinguistic Basis of the Linguistic Automaton," *International Journal of Psycholinguistics* 10, 1 (1994): 15–32.

4. Letter to Colonel Edward Carrington, Jan. 16, 1787, taken from *The Life and Writings of Thomas Jefferson,* eds. A. Koch and W. Peden (New York: Random House, 1944), pp. 411–12.

5. Roger Shattuck, "The Shame of the Schools," *New York Review of Books* 52, 6 (April 2005).

6. W. N. Francis and H. Kucera, *Frequency Analysis of English Usage: Lexicon and Grammar* (Boston: Houghton Mifflin, 1982).

7. John Willinsky, "The Vocabulary of Cultural Literacy in a Newspaper of Substance," ERIC, ED 302836 EDRS.

8. E. D. Hirsch, *Cultural Literacy* (Boston: Houghton Mifflin, 1987).

9. The Core Knowledge Sequence is available from the nonprofit Core Knowledge Foundation, 801 East High Street, Charlottesville, VA 22902, or on the Internet at www.coreknowledge.org.

5. USING SCHOOL TIME PRODUCTIVELY

1. E. D. Hirsch, Jr., "Reading Comprehension Requires Knowledge — of Words and the World," *American Educator* 27, 1 (Spring 2003): 10ff.

2. U.S. Department of Education, National Center for Educational Statistics, *Pursuing Excellence: Comparisons of International Eighth-Grade Mathematics and Science Achievement from a U.S. Perspective, 1995 and 1999,* http://nces.ed.gov/programs/coe/2002/section2/tables/t13_3.asp.

3. International Association for the Evaluation of Educational Achievement, *Progress in International Reading Literacy Study* (PIRLS), 2001; Organization for Economic Cooperation and Development, *Program for International Student Assessment* (PISA), 2000. See also Mariann Lemke . . . [et al.], U.S. Dept. of Education, *Outcomes of Learning Re-*

sults from the 2000 Program for International Student Assessment of 15-Year-Olds in Reading, Mathematics, and Science Literacy (Washington, D.C.: National Center for Education Statistics Educational Resources Information, 2001); Laurence T. Ogle et al., *International Comparisons in Fourth-Grade Reading Literacy: Findings from the Progress in International Reading Literacy Study (PIRLS) of 2001* (Washington, DC: National Center for Education Statistics, U.S. Dept. of Education, Institute of Education Sciences, 2003).

4. Harold W. Stevenson and James W. Stigler, *The Learning Gap: Why Our Schools Are Failing and What We Can Learn from Japanese and Chinese Education* (New York: Summit, 1992).

5. E. D. Hirsch, *The Schools We Need* (New York: Doubleday, 1996), pp. 38–41; Centre for Educational Research and Innovation, *Immigrant's Children at School* (Paris: Organization for Economic Cooperation and Development, 1987). For France in particular, see also S. Boulot and D. Boyden-Fradet, *Les Immigrés et l'école: une course d'obstacles* (Paris, 1988); M. Duthoit, "L'enfant et l'école: Aspects synthetiques du suivi d'un échantillon de vingt mille élèves des écoles," *Education et Formations* 16 (1988): 3–13.

6. Hirsch, *The Schools We Need*, pp. 22–26.

7. Sometimes the teacher, not knowing that dinosaurs and seeds were taught in the previous grade, teaches them again in the new grade — a different source of inefficiency.

8. Geraldine J. Clifford and James W. Guthrie, *Ed School: A Brief for Professional Education* (Chicago: University of Chicago Press, 1988); Diane Ravitch, *Left Back: A Century of Failed School Reforms* (New York: Simon & Schuster, 2000).

9. Betty Hart and Todd R. Risley, *Meaningful Differences in the Everyday Experience of Young American Children* (Baltimore: Peter Brookes, 1995), p. 58.

10. J. S. Coleman, *Equality and Achievement in Education* (San Francisco: Westview, 1990), pp. 29, 68, 163, 299.

11. Ibid., pp. 67–165.

12. Freddie D. Smith, "The Impact of the Core Knowledge Curriculum, A Comprehensive School Reform Model, On Achievement," Ph.D. dissertation, University of Virginia, 2003; "Summary of Research on the Effectiveness of Core Knowledge," http://www.coreknowledge.org/CK proto2/about/eval.htm.

13. See www.coreknowledge.org.

14. This research is translated and summarized on the Core Knowledge Web site: http://www.coreknowledge.org/CKproto2/Preschool/ preschool_frenchequity_frames.htm.

15. See J. S. Coleman, *Equality of Educational Opportunity* (Washington, D.C.: U.S. Government Printing Office, 1966).

16. Smith, "The Impact of the Core Knowledge Curriculum."

17. C. Schatschneider, J. Torgesen, et al., A Multivariate Study of Individual Differences in Performance on the Reading Portion of the Florida Comprehensive Assessment Test: A Preliminary Report, 2004, Florida Center for Reading Research, www.fcrr.org/TechnicalReports/Multi_ variate_Study_december2004.pdf.

18. If the very early tests were designed to measure students' *oral* comprehension of language, it is likely that the most critical factors in reading comprehension both early and late (given adequate decoding skill) would turn out to be students' word and world knowledge. This prediction is supported by Sticht's finding that early listening skill reliably predicts later reading skill. See Thomas G. Sticht et al., *Auding and Reading: A Developmental Model* (Alexandria, Va.: Human Resources Research Organization, July 1974), Technical Report. No. 74–36, p. 116.

6. USING TESTS PRODUCTIVELY

1. Donna R. Recht and Lauren Leslie, "Effect of Prior Knowledge on Good and Poor Readers' Memory of Text," *Journal of Educational Psychology* 80, 1 (Mar. 1988): 16–20.

2. E. D. Hirsch, "Measuring the Communicative Effectiveness of Prose," in J. Dominic, C. Fredricksen, and M. Whiteman, eds., *Writing* (Hillsdale, N.J.: Erlbaum, 1981), pp. 189–207. See also Recht and Leslie, "Effect of Prior Knowledge."

3. There is another source of unfairness in these state tests — the cut scores in the different states vary a good deal. This means that a student is deemed proficient in one state but would be deemed below proficient in another. I have been told by authorities in several states that reading cut scores are decided on *after* children take the tests, so the states can meet the political requirement for a reasonable number to pass and so the schools will not appear ineffectual. This variation in cut scores is definitely not the case for the congressionally mandated National Assessment of Educational Progress (NAEP) reading test.

The cut score between "proficient" and "below proficient" is carefully determined and is applied without favor to children in all states. We can compare NAEP results in a state with the state's own results and thus gain a calibration tool with which we can determine just how meaningful and fair the cut scores are in the different states. This discloses a very large variation. It is hard to say which kind of unfairness uncovered here is more deplorable — the unfairness that students in one state fail while students with the same reading abilities pass in another, or the unfairness of passing a student who cannot understand much of what he reads. See Jennifer Sloan McCombs, Sheila Nataraj Kirby, Heather Barney, Hilary Darilek, and Scarlett J. Magee, "Achieving State and National Literacy Goals, a Long Uphill Road: A Report to Carnegie Corporation of New York," TR-180-EDU (Santa Monica: Rand Corporation, 2004).

4. Ibid. See also P. E. Peterson and F. M. Hess, "Johnny Can Read . . . in Some States," *Education Next* (Summer 2005): 52–55.

5. See, for example, J. I. Brown, V. V. Fishco, and G. Hanna, *Nelson-Denny Reading Test*, Technical Report, Forms G & H, Riverside, Chicago, 1993; W. H. MacGinitie and R. K. MacGinitie, *Gates-MacGinitie Reading Tests*, 3rd ed., Technical Report, Riverside, Chicago, 1989.

6. William R. Johnson and Derek Neal, "Basic Skills and the Black-White Earnings Gap," in Christopher Jencks and Meredith Phillips, eds., *The Black-White Test Score Gap* (Washington, D.C.: Brookings Institution, 1998), pp. 480–97.

7. John B. Carroll, "Psychometric Approaches to the Study of Language Abilities," in C. J. Fillmore, D. Kempler, and S.-Y. Wang, eds., *Individual Differences in Language Abilities and Language Behavior* (New York: Academic, 1979).

8. J. Bishop, "The Impacts of Minimum Competency Exam Graduation Requirements on High School Graduation, College Attendance, and Early Labor Market Success," *Labour Economics* 8, 2 (2001): 203–22; J. Bishop and M. Bishop, "How External Exit Exams Spur Achievement," *Educational Leadership* 59, 1 (2001): 58–65.

9. G. Taylor and G. Kimball, "The Impact of Core Knowledge Implementation on Student Achievement in the Oklahoma City Public Schools," Occasional Papers, Oklahoma City Public Schools, May 2000, http://www.coreknowledge.org/CKproto2/about/eval/eval12_2002.htm; "Summary of Research on The Effectiveness of Core

Knowledge," http://www.coreknowledge.org/CKproto2/about/eval
.htm.

10. D. Lubinski and L. G. Humphreys, "Incorporating General Intelligence into Epidemiology and the Social Sciences," 24, 1 (1997): 159–202.
The positive correlation between achieved ability and socioeconomic
status is .422, whereas the correlation between achieved ability and
general information is .811.

7. ACHIEVING COMMONALITY AND FAIRNESS

1. Deborah Cohen, "Frequent Moves Said to Boost Risk of School Problems," *Education Week,* Sept. 22, p. 15. See also David Wood, Neal
Halfon, and Debra Scarlata, "Impact of Family Relocation on Children's Growth, Development, School Function, and Behavior," *Journal
of the American Medical Association* 270 (Sept. 15, 1993): 1334–38.

2. H. J. Walberg, "Improving Local Control and Learning," Preprint 1994.
Walberg cites B. C. Straits, "Residence, Migration, and School Progress," *Sociology of Education* 60 (1987): 34–43.

3. U.S. Census Bureau, *Annual Geographical Mobility Rates, by Type of
Movement: 1947–2000* (2001). http://www.census.gov/population/
www/socdemo/migrate.html.

4. U.S. Government Accounting Office, *Elementary School Children:
Many Change Schools Frequently, Harming Their Education,* GAO/
HEHS Publication No. 94–45 (Washington, D.C.: Government Print-
ing Office, 1994).

5. Deborah Cohen, "Moving Images," *Education Week,* Aug. 3, 1994, pp.
32–39; D. Kerbow, "Patterns of Urban Student Mobility and Local
School Reform," *Journal of Education for Students Placed At Risk* 1, 2
(1996); S. Pribesh and D. Downey, "Why Are Residential and School
Moves Associated with Poor School Performance?" *Demography* 36,
4 (1999): 521–34; T. Fowler-Finn, "Student Stability vs. Mobility,"
School Administrator 58, 7 (2001): 36–40; R. Rumberger, K. Larson,
R. Ream, and G. Palardy, "The Educational Consequences of Mobility
for California Students and Schools," PACE Policy Brief (Berkeley, Ca-
lif.: Policy Analysis for California Education, 1999); D. Stover, "The
Mobility Mess of Students Who Move," *Education Digest* 66, 3 (2000):
61–64.

6.   U.S. Government Accounting Office, "Elementary School Children."

7.   Ibid.

8.   Cohen, "Moving Images."

9.   Ibid.; Roger A. Johnson and Arnold H. Lindblad, "Effect of Mobility on Academic Performance of Sixth-Grade Students," *Perceptual and Motor Skills* 72 (Apr. 1991): 547–52; Gary M. Ingersoll, James P. Scamman, and Wayne D. Eckerling, "Geographic Mobility and Student Achievement in an Urban Setting (Denver Public Schools)," *Educational Evaluation and Policy Analysis* 11 (Summer 1989): 143–49.

10. E. D. Hirsch, Jr., *The Schools We Need* (New York: Doubleday, 1996).

11. Ibid., pp. 26–32.

12. D. Ravitch, *The Language Police: How Pressure Groups Restrict What Students Learn* (New York: Knopf, 2003).

13. Roger Shattuck, "The Shame of the Schools," *New York Review of Books* 52, 6 (Apr. 2005).

14. The Core Knowledge Foundation has provided a document for each state showing how its schools can follow state standards and at the same time teach a real curriculum, Core Knowledge, without doing extra work.

15. E. D. Hirsch, *The Schools We Need*, p. 29.

16. A. D. Benner, *The Cost of Teacher Turnover* (Austin: Texas Center for Educational Research, 2000), http://www.sbec.state.tx.us/SBEC/Online/turnoverrpt.pdf.

17. B. Rowan, R. Corenti, and R. J. Richard, "What Large-Scale Research Tells Us about Teacher Effects on Student Achievement" (Philadelphia: Consortium for Policy Research on Education, U. of Pennsylvania, 2002), http://www.cpre.org/Publications/rr51.pdf.

18. M. H. Abel and J. Sewell, "Stress and Burnout in Rural and Urban Secondary School Teacher," *Journal of Educational Research* 92, 5 (1999): 23–35.

19. S. Black, "When Teachers Feel Good About Their Work, Student Achievement Rises," *American School Board Journal* (Jan. 2001).

20. H. Stevenson and J. Stigler, *The Learning Gap: Why Our Schools Are Failing and What We Can Learn from Japanese and Chinese Education* (New York: Summit, 1992), p. 196.

21. J. Bruner, *The Process of Education* (Cambridge, Mass.: Harvard University Press, 1960), p. 33.

22. W. C. Bagley, *Education and Emergent Man: A Theory of Education*

with *Particular Application to Public Education in the United States* (New York: Nelson, 1934), p. 139.

APPENDIX: THE CRITICAL IMPORTANCE OF AN ADEQUATE THEORY OF READING

1. S. Weinberg, *Dreams of a Final Theory* (New York: Pantheon, 1992), pp. 257–58.
2. J. Mervis, "Meager Evaluations Make It Hard to Find Out What Works," *Science* 11, 304 (June 2004): 1583.
3. H. P. Grice, "Logic and Conversation," in *Studies in the Way of Words* (Cambridge, Mass.: Harvard University Press, 1989). This was the title of a series of seven William James Lectures that Grice delivered at Harvard University in 1967–68, widely circulated in typescript.
4. J. Habermas, *On the Pragmatics of Social Interaction: Preliminary Studies in the Theory of Communicative Action*, B. Fultner, trans. (Cambridge, Mass.: MIT Press, 2001).
5. Barak Rosenshine and Carla Meister, "Reciprocal Teaching: A Review of the Research," *Review of Educational Research* 64, 4 (Winter 1994): 479–530.
6. Keith E. Stanovich and Paula J. Stanovich, *Using Research and Reason in Education: How Teachers Can Use Scientifically Based Research to Make Curricular and Instructional Decisions* (Washington, D.C.: U.S. Department of Education, 2003); Keith E. Stanovich and Paula J. Stanovich, "How Research Might Inform the Debate about Early Reading Acquisition," *Journal of Research in Reading* 18, 2 (Sept. 1995): 87–105. It would be unfortunate if "random assignment" were thought to be a uniquely royal road to educational improvement. Random assignment of subjects is machinery, just as use of statistics is machinery. If the experiments themselves aren't long-term, and if the interventions being studied aren't based on the best theoretical principles, they will be unlikely to foster educational improvement merely because the experiments are punctilious. The theoretical advantage of randomized trials lies in their probable lack of bias. In many cases, computerized matched-pair analyses from the archives might be even more informative when the analysis is carried out with a greater number of students. Such analysis carries the additional advantage of not requiring a wait of five years in order to gauge long-term effects.

7. A. Einstein, "Ueber das Relativitaetsprinzip und die aus demselben gezogenen Folgerungen," *Jahrbuch der Radioactivitaet und Elektronik* 4 (1907): 411–62. See also M. Taper and R. L. Subhash, eds., *The Nature of Scientific Evidence: Statistical, Philosophical, and Empirical Considerations* (Chicago: University of Chicago Press, 2004).

8. Weinberg, *Dreams of a Final Theory,* pp. 62–63.

Acknowledgments

I am very grateful for the excellent advice I have received from the following people who read and commented in detail on the entire manuscript: Matthew Davis, Ted Hirsch, Elizabeth McPike, Robert Shepherd, Keith Stanovich, and Deanne Urmy. I am also grateful for comments by Barbara Garvin-Kester, Polly Hirsch, Gloria Loomis, Diane Ravitch, Louisa Spencer, and Daniel Willingham. My intellectual debts branch out in so many directions that it would be idle to attempt a listing of them, but I wish to express particular gratitude to two writers whose scientific works have been of special value, George A. Miller and Walter Kintsch.

INDEX

academic intensity, 86–87
achievement gap. *See also* disadvantaged children; "Matthew effect" in reading
  content standards and, 105
  between demographic groups, 2–3, 86–87
  as knowledge problem, 25–26, 74
  NCLB activity and, 18–19
  social goals and, 15
  U.S. vs. other countries and, 1–2, 82, 86
Adams, Marilyn Jager, 23
alphabet, 63–64
American Educator (journal), 23, 123
American Federation of Teachers, 123
Anderson, Richard, 65
anticontent ideas, 112–13. *See also* comprehension strategies; formalism
anti-intellectualism, 9–10
Aristotle, 37
Arizona, 16

assumed knowledge. *See* background knowledge; shared knowledge; taken-for-granted knowledge

background knowledge. *See also* "domain-specific" knowledge; shared knowledge
  anti-intellectualism and, 10
  baseball example and, 68–69
  class time and, 81–82
  core content in early grades and, 119–24
  cultural literacy and, 6
  curriculum content and, 43–45
  disparagement of "facts" and, 8–10
  effects of deficits in, 10–11
  general vs. specific, 43
  as individual, 40–42
  language comprehension and, 34, 35–39
  Martian example and, 71
  "Matthew" effect and, 25–26, 34–35

161

background knowledge (*cont.*)
  mental speed and, 97–98
  nature of knowledge needed and, 74–77
  NCLB and, 21–22
  newspapers and, 73–74
  sentence comprehension and, 68–70
  strategies and, 47–48, 97–98
  types of, 39–45
Bagley, William, 120
Bank Street School of Education (New York City), 40–41
Bernstein, Basil, 56–58, 69
Bishop, John, 105
blame-society theory, 14–16, 83
blank spaces, and language comprehension, 37–39
book learning
  factual knowledge and, 10–11
  pre-romantic tradition and, 9
boredom
  comprehension strategies and, 45–50
  curricular incoherence and, 116–18
broad knowledge. *See* background knowledge
Brown Corpus, 75
Bruner, Jerome, 119–20
Burt Dow: Deep-Water Man (McCloskey), 70

California, 16, 80–81, 129
California Test of Basic Skills (CTBS), 100
Chall, Jeanne, 23, 25, 78
class time
  comprehension strategies and, 12–14

current allocation for reading, 16
  effective use of, 88–90
  opportunity cost and, 80–83
  vocabulary learning and, 61–62
Clifford, Geraldine, 20
cognitive science, and comprehension, 17, 130–32
Coleman, James, 86–87
Columbia University Teachers College, 20
commonality
  decline of, 107–8
  democratic ideals and, 108–9
  myth of local curriculum and, 111–12
comprehension strategies, 45–50. *See also* process orientation; reading comprehension
  class example of, 12–14
  formalism and, 11–14
  initial effects of, 49
  standardized testing and, 94, 95–96
  textual understanding and, 36–37
  theory behind, 130–32
  types of, 12
computer translation, 71
conservative tradition, 112–13, 127–28, 134
convergence, principle of, 134–36
conversational speech, vs. formal speech, 32–34
core content
  advantages to specifying, 115–19
  in early grades, 119–24
  indoctrination issue and, 113–14
Core Knowledge Sequence
  curriculum and, 77–78, 123
  effectiveness and, 88, 89
  Web site for, 151n13

criterion-referenced tests, 99, 100, 101

critical thinking, 11–12, 45–47, 114, 139n19. *See also* comprehension strategies; formalism

CTBS. *See* California Test of Basic Skills (CTBS)

Cultural Literacy (Hirsch), 6

culture
  anticontent ideas and, 122
  blame-society theory and, 14–16, 83
  polarization and, 107–8
  standardized testing and, 98
  textual comprehension and, 68–69, 72

Cunningham, Anne, 61

curriculum content
  Core Knowledge Sequence and, 77–78, 89–90
  incoherence of, 83–85, 116–19
  language arts classes and, 78–79, 88
  localism and, 112–14
  in other countries, 110
  process orientation in, 112–13, 114
  reading as separate and, 12–14, 42–43
  teacher effectiveness and, 83–85
  testing and, 102, 104–5
  value of coherence in, 78–79, 81–83, 108

cut scores, 99, 152n3

Darwin, Charles, 58

data-gathering, 128–29, 130

decoding (phonics)
  achievements in, 23–26, 28

naturalistic approach and, 8, 23
  NCLB activity and, 19
  reading skill and, 24–25, 28, 35–36

democracy, 74, 107
  early education and, 108–9, 120
  fairness and, 85–87
  indoctrination and, 113–14

demographic determinism, 15–16, 22, 110. *See also* disadvantaged children; parental education

determinism. *See* demographic determinism

development, as term, 5–6, 138n9

Dewey, John, 5–6, 9–10

disadvantaged children
  achievement gap and, 1, 2–3, 18, 96
  core curriculum and, 123–24
  mobility problem and, 109–12, 119–21
  standardized testing and, 97–98
  use of school time and, 85–87
  vocabulary building and, 66–67

"domain-specific" knowledge. *See also* background knowledge
  mental models and, 17
  reading ability and, 12, 37–39

early education. *See also* early grades; preschools; toddler years
  delayed effects and, 89, 132
  democratic ideal and, 108–9
  in France, 88–89

early grades
  core content in, 119–24
  oral language and, 26–27, 34–35, 49–50
  reading tests and, 104
  self-reading skill and, 27

Ebonics, 53, 55

educational organizations, 123–24
educational philosophy
    blame-society approach and, 14–
        16, 83
    conflict of ideas in, 20–21, 130–36
    conservative-liberal debate in,
        127–28, 134
    formalism and, 11–14, 20–21
    localism and, 112–14
    romanticism and, 3–5
    scientific evidence and, 14, 128–29
educational reform, 20
educational research
    NCLB legislation and, 18–22
    need for theory in, 128–30
    Tennessee STAR study and, 128–
        29
education schools. See teacher edu-
    cation
Edwards, Jonathan, 4, 5
Einstein, Albert, 131, 135
elaborated code vs. restricted code,
    56–58, 69
elaboration, 29, 85–86
Emerson, Ralph Waldo, 4, 5, 9
enthymeme, 37
equity. See fairness

factual knowledge. See background
    knowledge
fairness. See also demographic de-
    terminism; disadvantaged chil-
    dren
    academic intensity and, 86–87
    curricular incoherence and, 118–
        19
    cut scores and, 99, 152n3
    democracy and, 85–87, 109

    early education and, 108–9, 119–
        24
    standardized testing and, 97–98
fiction, 79
Florida
    FCAT and, 101
    testing guidelines in, 94
    test questions in, 95
Ford, Henry, 9
formalism. See also comprehension
    strategies; process orientation
    comprehension strategies and, 11–
        14
    content of reading programs and,
        42–45
    ideology vs. theory and, 133–34
    reform and, 20–21
    testing policy and, 105–6
fourth-grade slump, 10–11
France, preschools in, 88–89

Gates-MacGinitie Reading Tests,
    100
general reading skill. See also read-
    ing comprehension
    and standardized tests, 36–37
Georgia, 16
gradualism
    standardized testing and, 89–90,
        104
    theoretical understanding of, 132–
        33
grammar
    learning of, 54–56, 59
    oral dialects and, 52–53
Grice, H. P., 130
growth, as term, 5–6
Guthrie, James, 20

Halpern, Diane, 140n19
Hart, Betty, 85–86
Herman, Patricia, 65
Highland Elementary School,
    Maryland, 12–14, 19
Hofstadter, Richard, 9
home speech
    respect for diversity and, 55–56
    vs. school speech, 51–54
how-to knowledge. *See* formalism

implicit-explicit learning debate,
    61–66
indoctrination
    core content and, 113–14
    teachers and, 114
inferences
    background knowledge and, 37–
        39, 48
    "inferencing" as strategy and,
        45–50, 97, 99
    scientific data and, 135–36
inflection, 52–53
instructional materials, 17. *See also*
    reading programs
instructional methods, efficiency
    of, 131
international comparisons
    Japan and, 140n23
    U.S. achievement gap and, 1–2, 14
Iowa Test of Basic Skills (ITBS),
    100, 101, 103
ITBS. *See* Iowa Test of Basic Skills
    (ITBS)

Japan, comparisons with, 140n23
Jefferson, Thomas, 3, 9, 10, 74, 108
Jesperson, Otto, 53

Johnson, Dr. Samuel, 52
Joseph, Marion, 24, 25

Kett, Joseph, 75
Keynes, John Maynard, 4
knowledge deficit
    achievement gap in U.S. and, 1–3
    anti-intellectualism and, 8–11
    blame-society theory and, 14–16, 83
    formalism in reading and, 11–14
    reading as unnatural and, 7–8
    romantic ideas and, 3–6
knowledge-oriented reading pro-
    gram. *See also* Core Knowledge
    Sequence
    demand for, 17–18
    other school subjects and, 108

Labov, William, 57
Landauer, Thomas, 64
language arts classes. *See also* curricu-
    lum content
    curriculum coherence and, 78–79, 88
    required time in, 80–81
    state curriculum guidelines and,
        115–16
language knowledge. *See also* Stan-
    dard English
    elaborated vs. restricted code and,
        56–58
    grammar and, 54–56
    print code and, 51–54
    vocabulary building and, 58–66
Learning Gap, The (Stevenson and
    Stigler), 118
Learning to Read: The Great Debate
    (Adams and Chall), 23
liberal tradition, 112–13, 127–28

listening skill, 26–35, 151n17. *See also* oral language
localism, 112–14
Lorentz, H. A., 135
Lyon, Reid, 23

"main idea," 46–47, 49, 99
Mann, Horace, 5, 108–9
Marshall, John (Chief Justice), 44
Massachusetts, 115
math achievement, 81–83
math learning, 7–8
"Matthew" effect in reading
  background knowledge and, 25–26, 34–35
  vocabulary and, 60–61, 66–67
Mayflower, teaching the, 119–22
McCloskey, Robert, 70
McGuffey Readers, 78
McPike, Elizabeth, 23
meaning
  unspoken, 37–39, 68–70, 130
  of words, 25, 44, 62–63, 64–65
mental speed, and background knowledge, 97–98
"metacognitive skills," 47–50. *See also* comprehension strategies
Miller, George A., 64–65
Milton, John, 9, 10, 139n15
mobility problem, 109–12, 119–21

NAEP scores. *See* National Assessment of Educational Progress (NAEP) scores
Nagy, William, 65
National Assessment of Educational Progress (NAEP) scores, 143n22, 152n3

National Council of Teachers of English (NCTE), 55, 145n3
natural, as term, 5–6, 7
naturalism
  ideology vs. theory and, 133–34
  reform and, 20–21
  as romantic idea, 3–6
  vocabulary building and, 63, 148n26
newspapers, and general knowledge, 73–74
New York City, 16, 80–81
New York State
  examples of questions in, 95
  testing guidelines in, 93–94
New York Times, background knowledge and, 73–74, 76
Nixon tapes, 32–33
No Child Left Behind law (NCLB)
  complaints against, 91–92
  educational philosophy and, 18–22
  standardized testing and, 91, 103–4
  yearly progress assessment and, 6, 18–19, 103–4
"norm-referenced" tests, 98–99, 100, 101

opportunity cost
  class time and, 80–83
  educational research and, 129, 131
oral class presentations, 31–32
oral language
  dialects and, 52–54
  early grades and, 26–27, 34–35, 49–50
  elaborated code vs. restricted code and, 56–58, 69
  need for traditional knowledge and, 122–23

reading skill and, 26–35
school speech vs. home speech
    and, 51–54
Organization for Economic Coop-
    eration and Development, 84

parental education
    decoding and, 24
    elaborated talk and, 85–86
Parrington, Vernon, 4
Pauli, Wolfgang, 127
Perlstein, Linda, 12–14, 19, 96
phonics. *See* decoding (phonics)
"phonological loop," 28, 34
Pinker, Steven, 59
Planck, Max, 14
poverty. *See* disadvantaged children
prepping, 92, 102
preschools, 88–89. *See also* toddler
    years
print code, learning of, 51–54. *See
    also* Standard English
problem-solving, 11. *See also* for-
    malism
process orientation. *See also* com-
    prehension strategies
    and curriculum content, 112–13,
    114, 116–17
progressivism
    how-to knowledge and, 11–12
    as term, 5–6

radio speech
    examples of, 30–32
    vs. ordinary talk, 29–30
    writing proficiency and, 30, 71–
    72
random assignment, 134–35, 155n6
Ravitch, Diane, 20

reading
    gradualism and, 132–33
    as natural, 4, 5
    as unnatural, 7–8
reading aloud, 29, 61. *See also* listen-
    ing skill
reading comprehension. *See also*
    comprehension strategies
    decoding and, 24–25, 35–36
    fourth-grade slump and, 10–11
    language comprehension and, 130
    listening skill and, 26–35, 151n17
    nature of, 96
    vocabulary growth and, 59–66
    word meaning and, 25, 44
reading programs
    content of, 42–43, 77–79
    scientific knowledge and, 17
    taken-for-granted knowledge and,
    70–71, 72
reading tests, nature of, 96–102. *See
    also* standardized testing
repetitiousness, 116, 117, 118
replicability, 128–29
Risley, Todd, 85–86
romantic ideas. *See also* naturalism
    knowledge deficit in U.S. and, 3–6
    NCLB and, 20–21
    teacher education and, 14, 16, 20
    unnaturalness of reading and, 7–8
rote learning, 10
Rothstein, Richard, 15–16

SAT scores, verbal, 2, 143n22
school mobility rate, 110–11. *See also*
    mobility problem
schools
    academic intensity and, 86–87
    effects of migration among, 109–12

school speech vs. home speech, 51–54

"self-monitoring" skills, 45–50, 131–32

sentence comprehension, background knowledge and, 68–70

Shakespeare, William, 8

shared knowledge. *See also* background knowledge; taken-for-granted knowledge

  communication with strangers and, 44–45

  general readers and, 70–72, 74–77

  restricted vs. elaborated code and, 56–58, 68–70

Shattuck, Roger, 115

situation model

  comprehension and, 17, 38–39, 43

  as term, 143n26

  vocabulary building and, 60

Smith, F. D., 89

social equity. *See* fairness

social justice goals, and achievement gap, 15, 21–22

specific background knowledge. *See* background knowledge

speech community, idea of, 122–23, 130

spoken language. *See* oral language; strangers, communication with

Standard English. *See also* language knowledge

  formal vs. informal speech and, 56–58

  grammar and, 54–56

  oral dialects and, 52–54

  origin of, 51–52

  print code and, 51–54

standardized testing

  delayed effects and, 89–90, 104

  disadvantaged children and, 97–98

  examples of materials in, 95, 96–97, 101

  flaws in state guidelines for, 93–96

  frequency of, 92

  general knowledge and, 36–37

  improvement of policy on, 104–5

  jargon and, 98–99

  as measure of progress, 102–3

  nationwide vs. state tests and, 100–101

  nature of reading tests and, 96–102

  NCLB and, 91–92

  prepping and, 92, 102

  provision of context in, 97

  referencing and, 99–102

  teaching of strategies and, 94–96

Stanovich, Keith, 61

state guidelines

  core content and, 123–24

  curriculum standards and, 113–14, 115–19, 121

  as empty, 98–100, 116–17

  scoring and, 99–101

  testing flaws and, 93–96

Sticht, Thomas G., 28, 151n17

strangers, communication with. *See also* Standard English

  assumed knowledge and, 44–45, 122–23

  elaborated code and, 56–58

  reading comprehension and, 30–35

  standard language and, 55

taken-for-granted knowledge. *See also* background knowledge; shared knowledge
need to teach, 121–22
reading programs and, 70–71, 72
speech community and, 130
teacher education
anticontent ideas and, 112
anti-intellectualism and, 10–11
curricular incoherence and, 83–85
individual knowledge and, 40–42
romantic ideas and, 14, 16, 20, 84–85
teachers
indoctrination and, 114
job satisfaction and, 117–19
quality of, 83–85
television. *See also* listening skill
speech comprehension and, 29, 71
time spent watching, 14, 140n23
Tennessee STAR study (Student Achievement Teacher Ratio), 128–29, 131
testing policy, 104–5
Texas
examples of questions in, 95
testing guidelines in, 93
theory of reading, need for, 127–36
Thoreau, Henry David, 4, 5
toddler years, 85–86. *See also* preschools

Torgesen, Joseph, 89
Trefil, James, 75

unspoken meaning, 37–39, 68–70, 130. *See also* background knowledge

vocabulary building, 58–66
disadvantaged children and, 66–67
familiarity of context and, 81
implicit-explicit learning debate and, 61–66
"Matthew" effect and, 60–61, 66–67
naturalism and, 63, 148n26
word-learning process and, 59–60

Walberg, Herbert, 110
Walsh, Kate, 45
Wattenberg, Ruth, 123
Weinberg, Steven, 135
What Your Second Grader Needs to Know (Hirsch), 38
"why" questions, 48–49
word frequencies, 75
word-learning capacity, 64–65. *See also* vocabulary building
word meaning, 25, 44, 62–63, 64–65, 75
Wordsworth, William, 9

yearly progress assessment, 6, 18–19, 103–4. *See also* standardized testing

© CORE KNOWLEDGE

E. D. Hirsch, Jr., is a professor emeritus of education
and humanities at the University of Virginia. He is
the author of many acclaimed books, including the
best-selling *Cultural Literacy* and the New York Times
Notable Book *The Schools We Need and Why We Don't
Have Them,* as well as the popular Core Knowledge
series, which includes *What Your First Grader Needs
to Know.*

In 1986, Hirsch founded the nonprofit Core
Knowledge Foundation to promote excellence and fair-
ness in early education. All of his proceeds from *The
Knowledge Deficit* will go to this foundation.

Hirsch is a member of both the American Academy
of Arts and Sciences and the International Academy
of Education. He has served on the Research Advisory
Board of the U.S. Department of Education and has
been a senior fellow of the National Endowment for
the Humanities. In 1997, the American Federation of
Teachers honored him with the Biennial Quest Award
for Outstanding Contribution to Education.